B&W Portfolio 2017

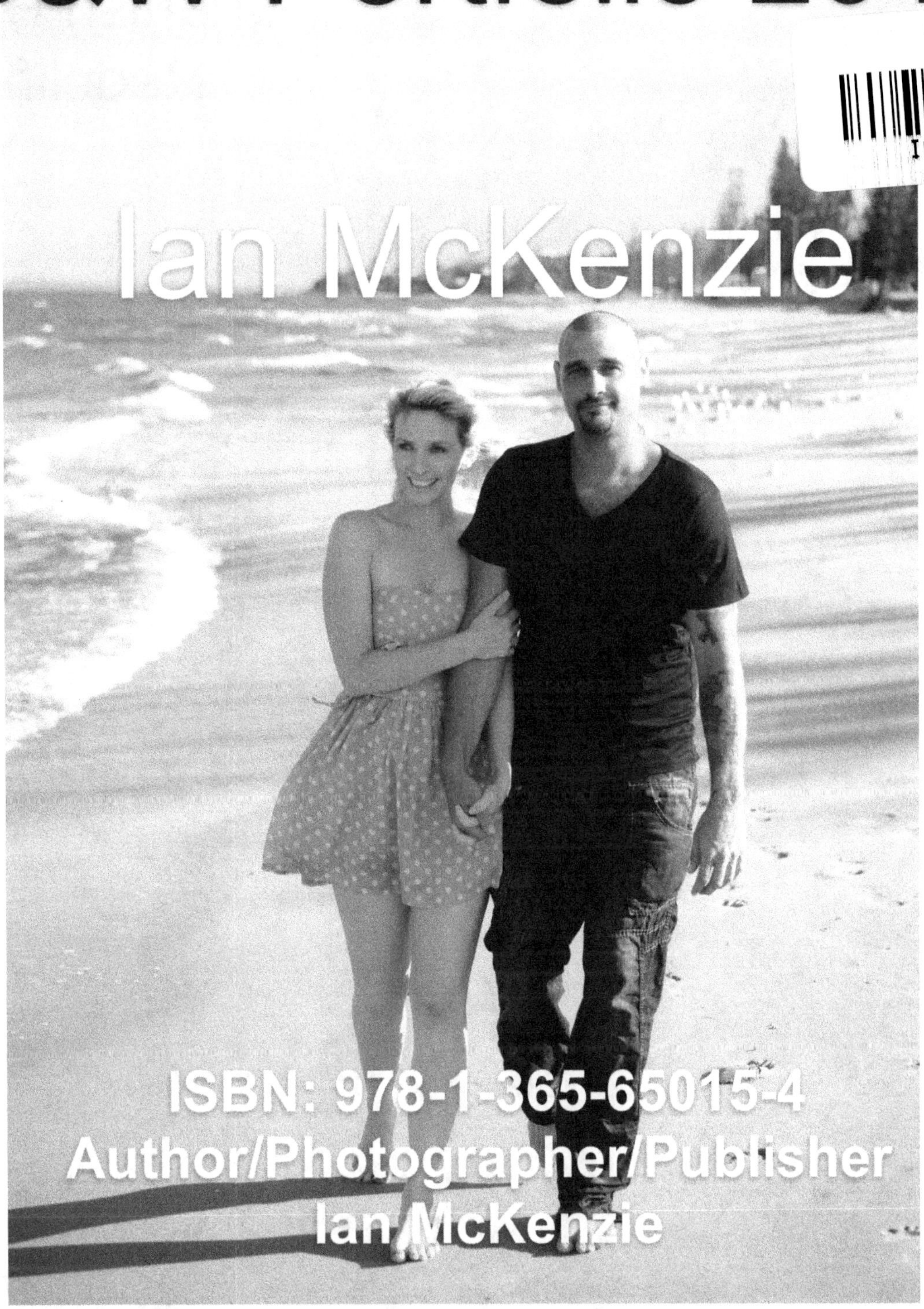

Ian McKenzie

ISBN: 978-1-365-65015-4
Author/Photographer/Publisher
Ian McKenzie

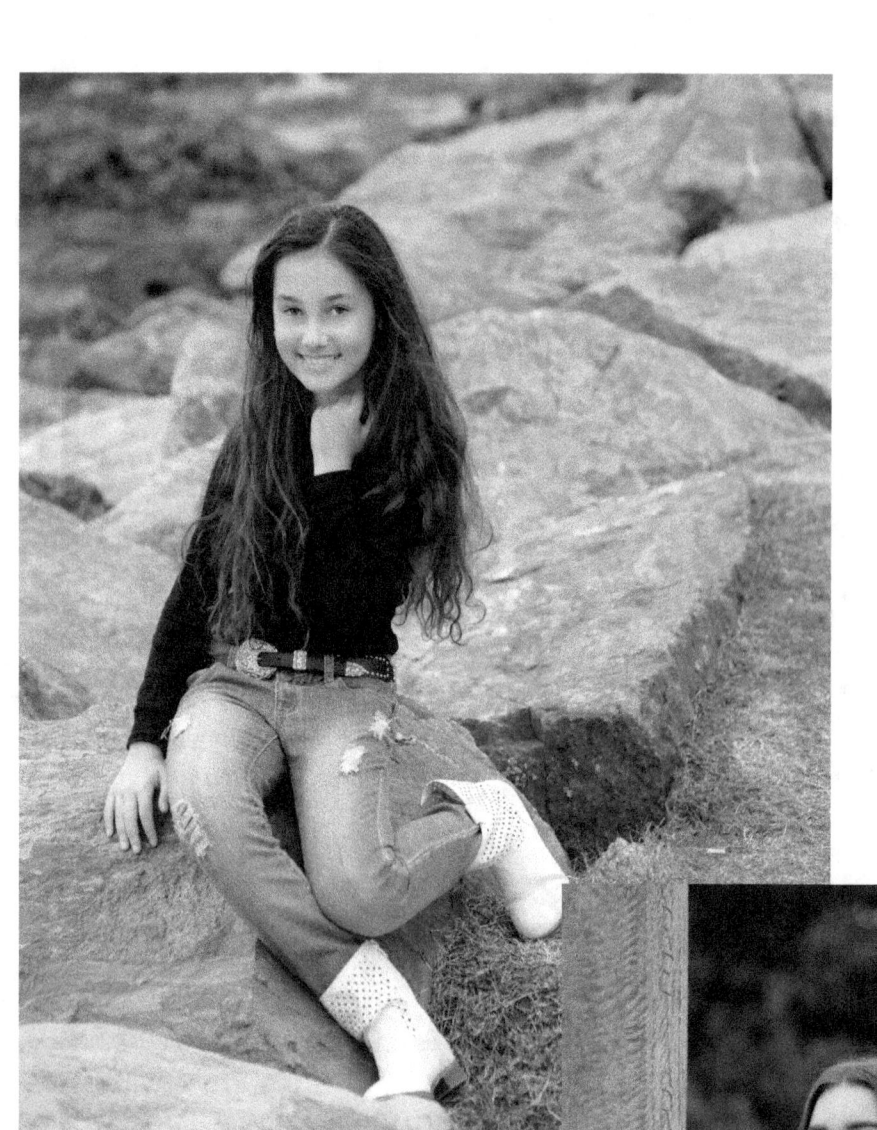

Charlish Park
Redcliffe

page 2

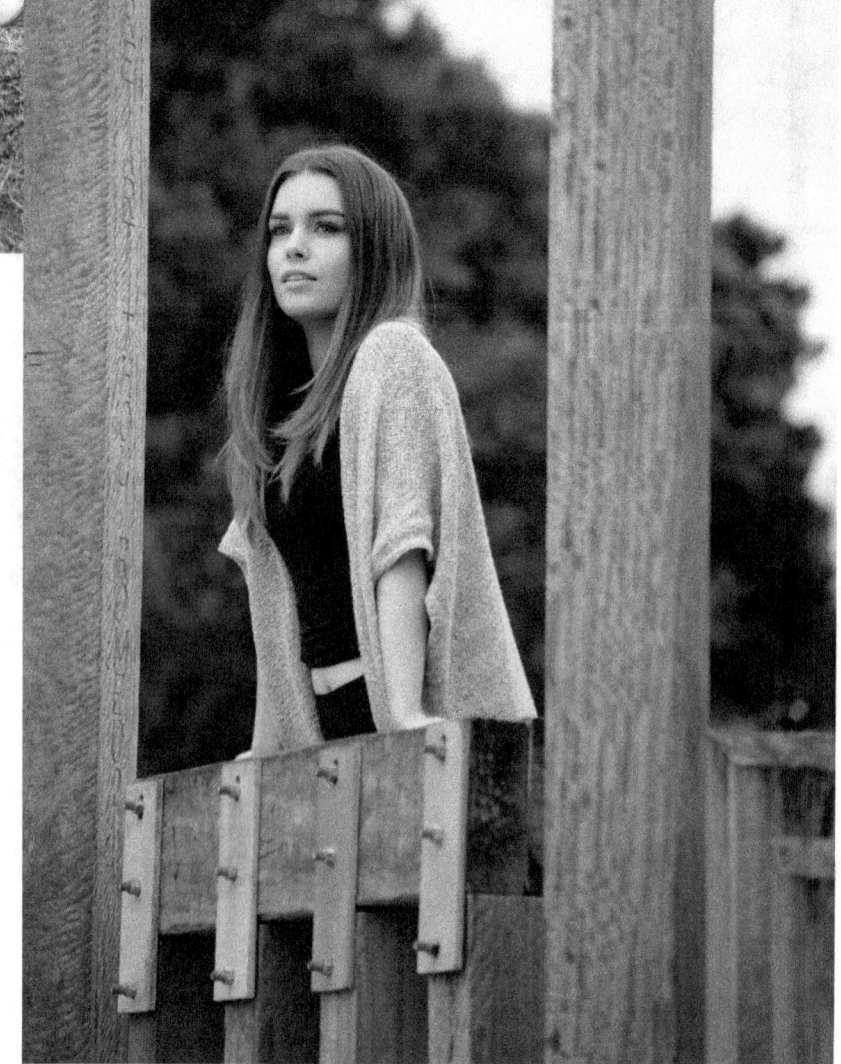

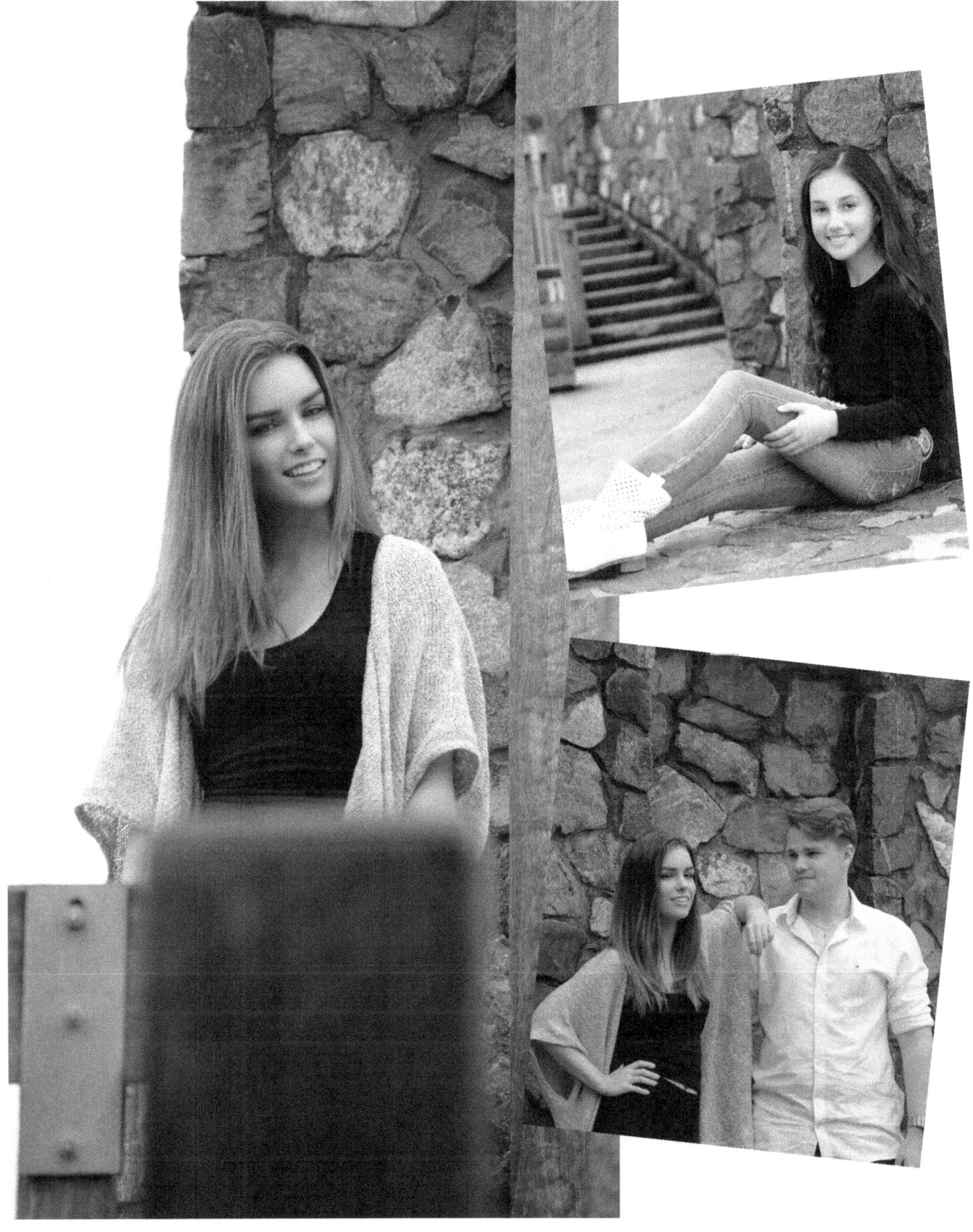

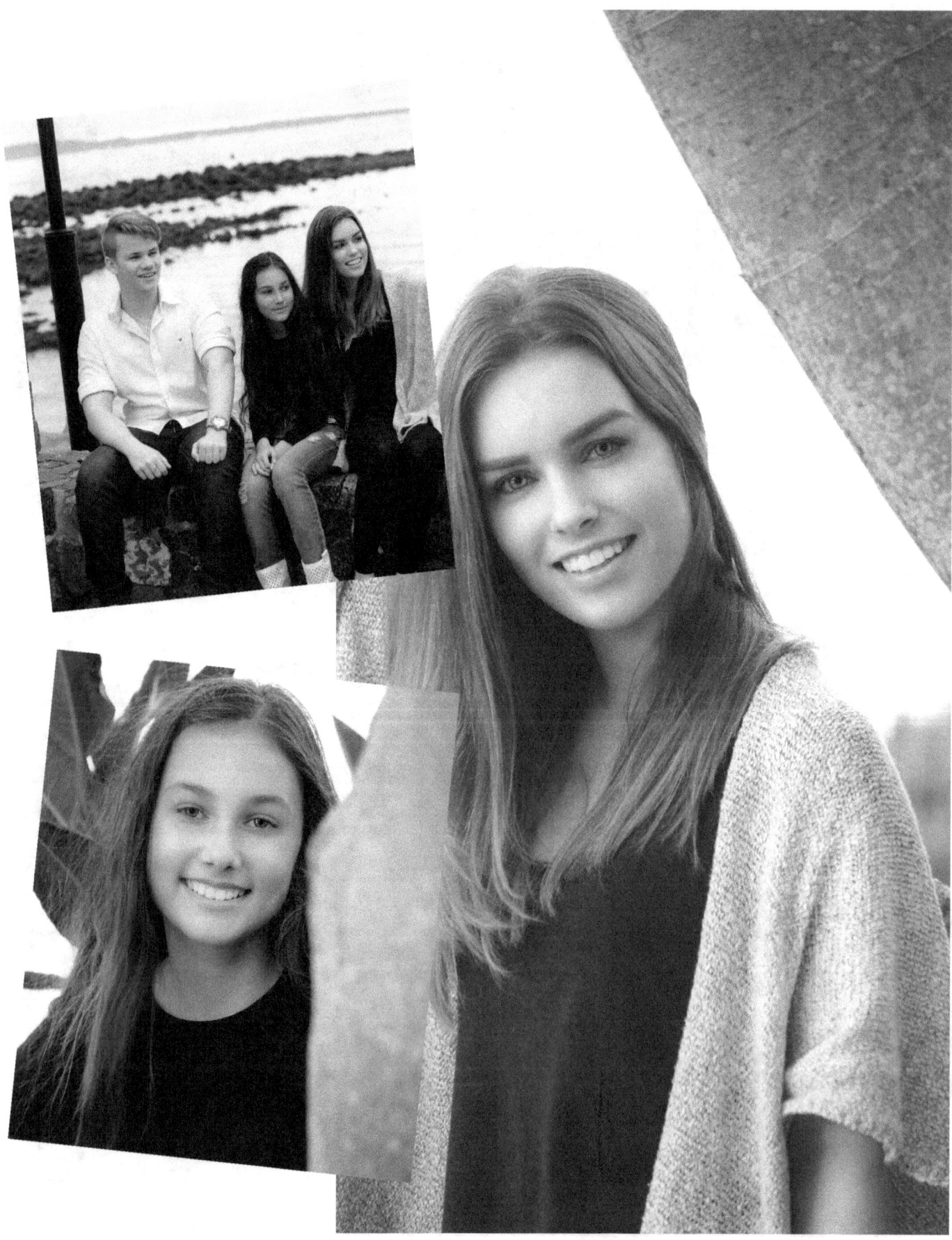

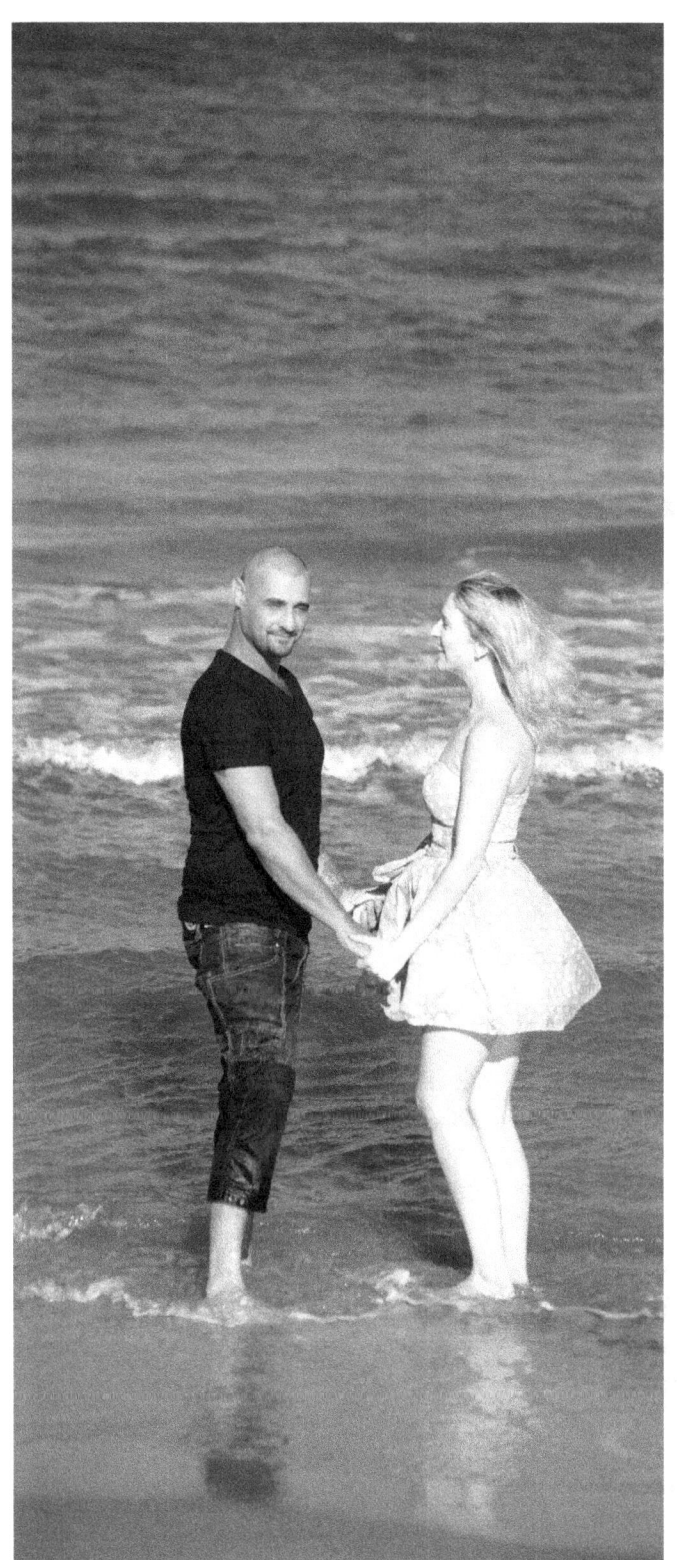

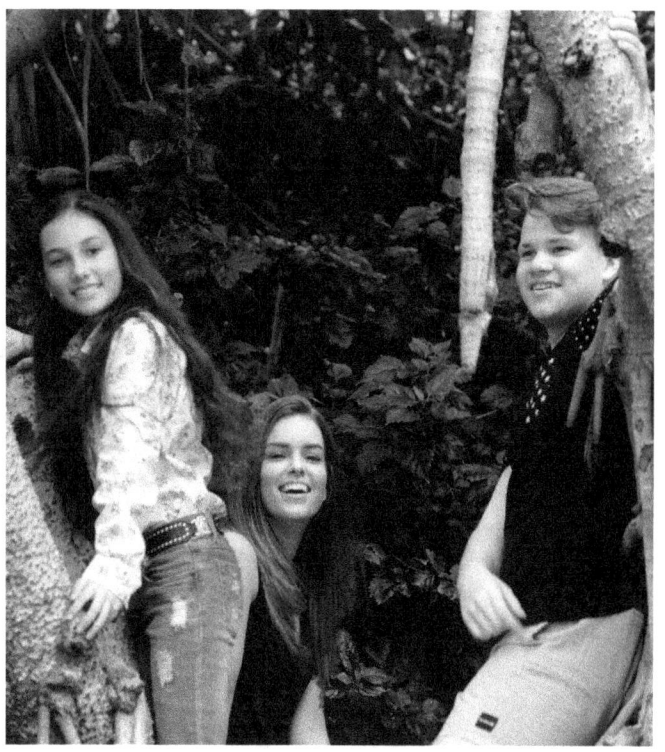

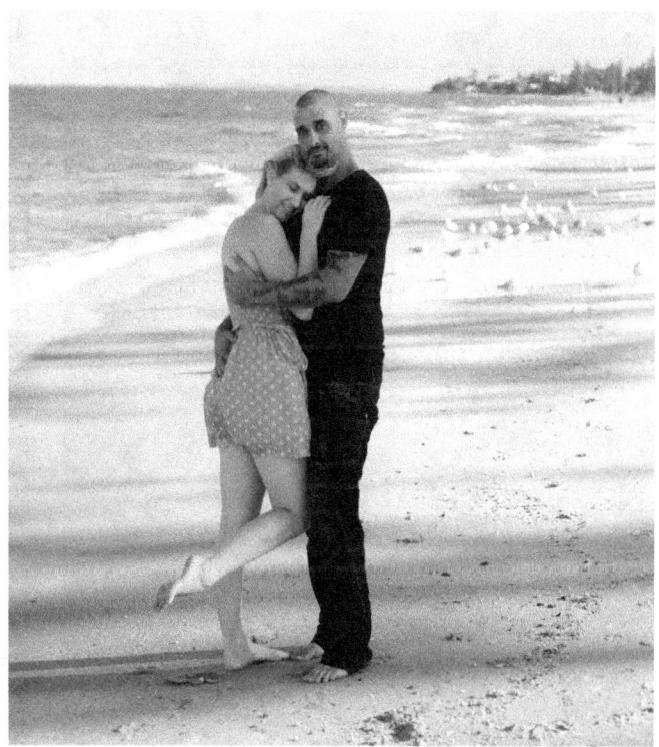

Suttons Beach Redcliffe

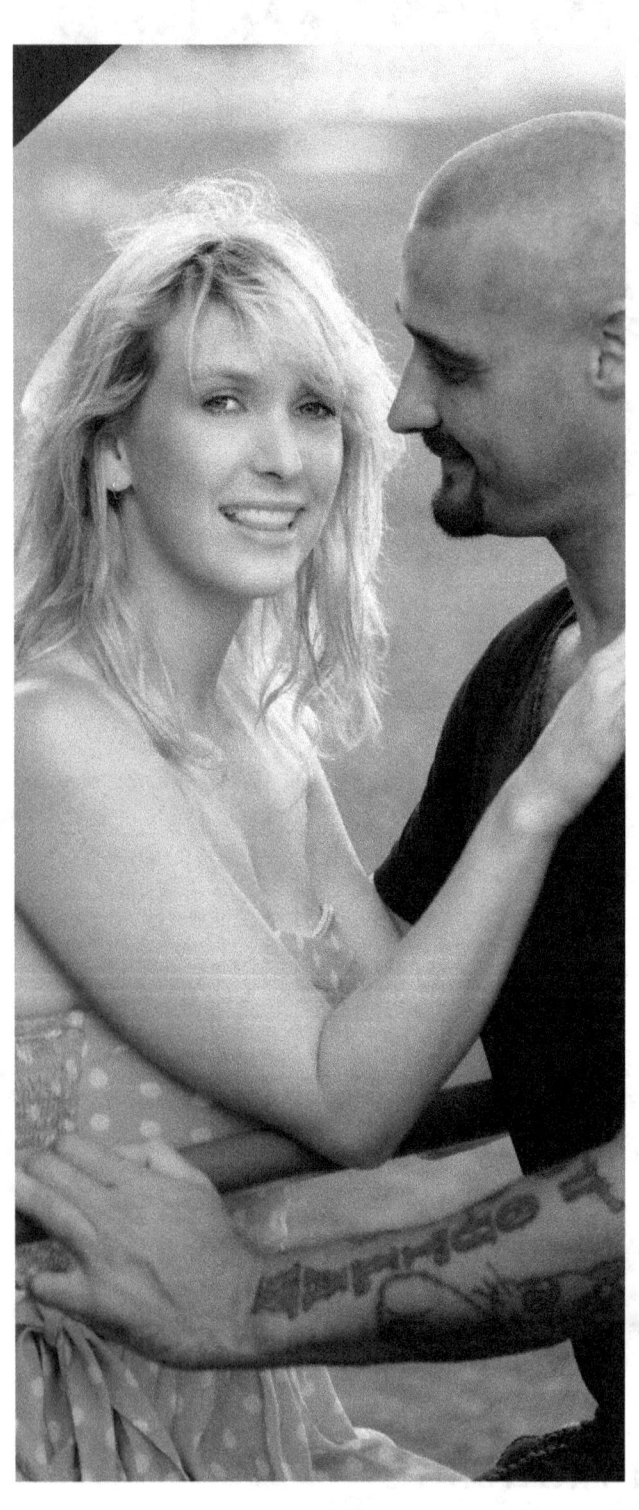

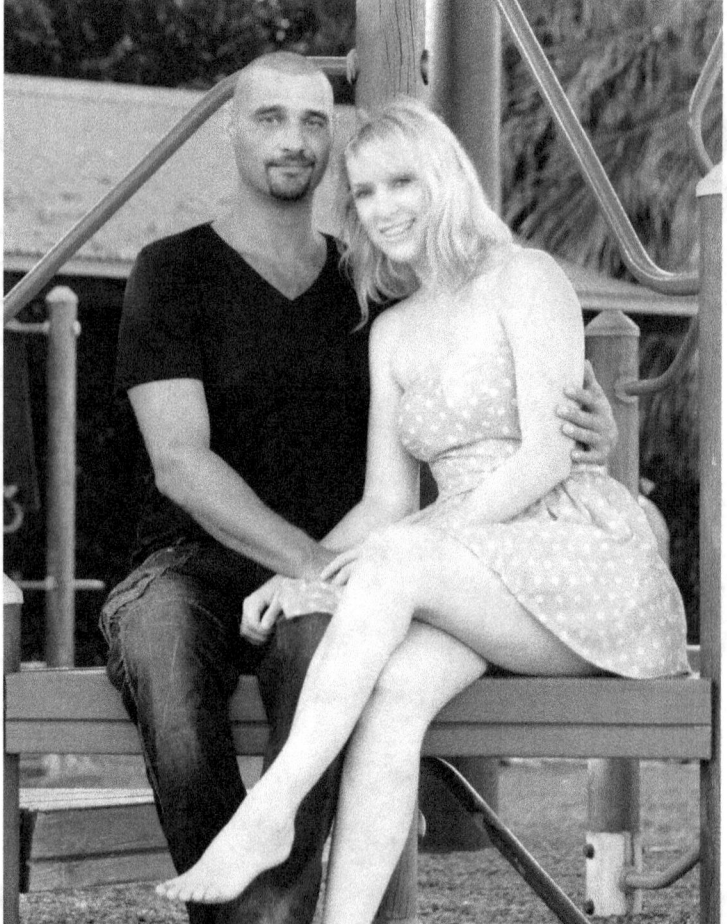

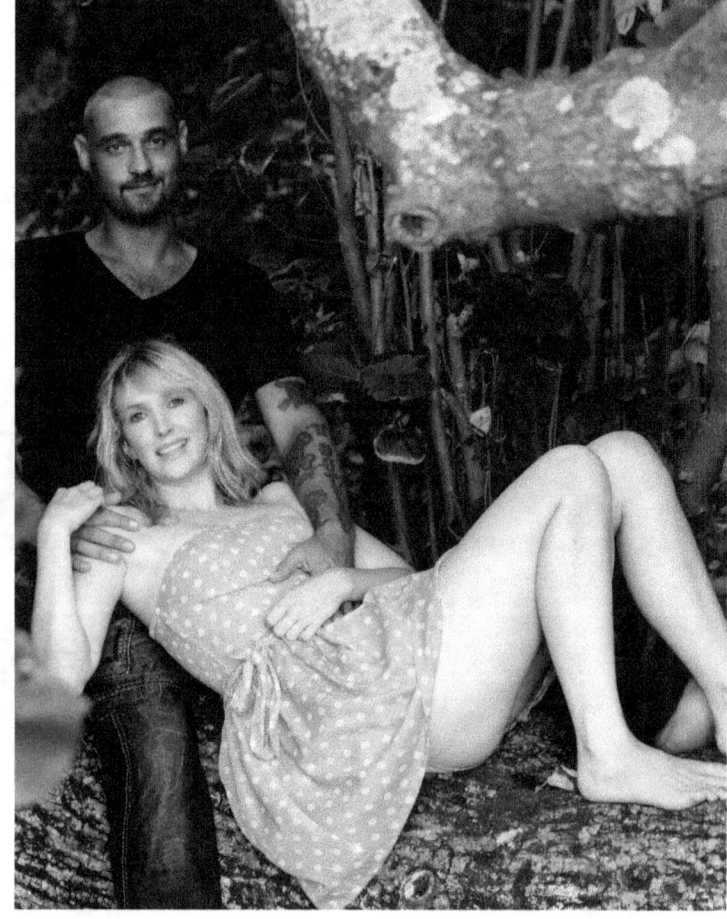

page 6

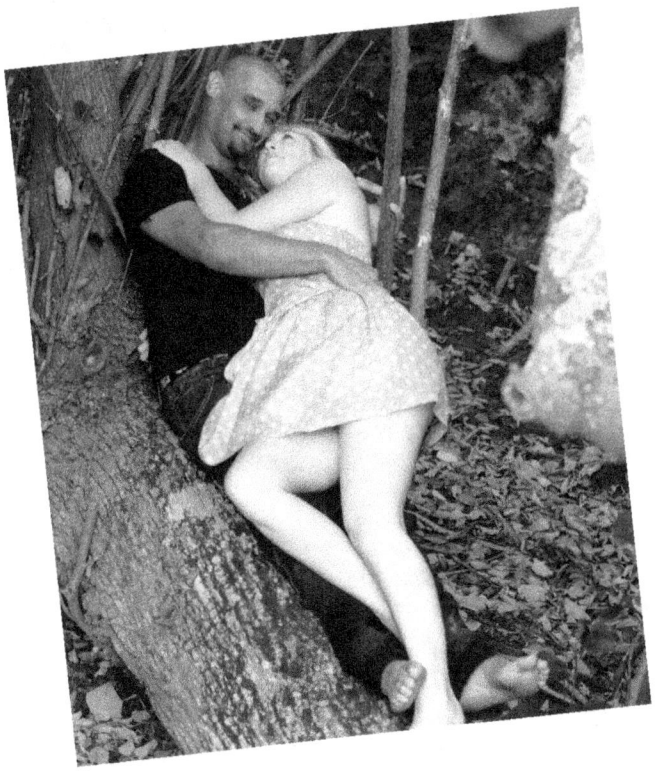 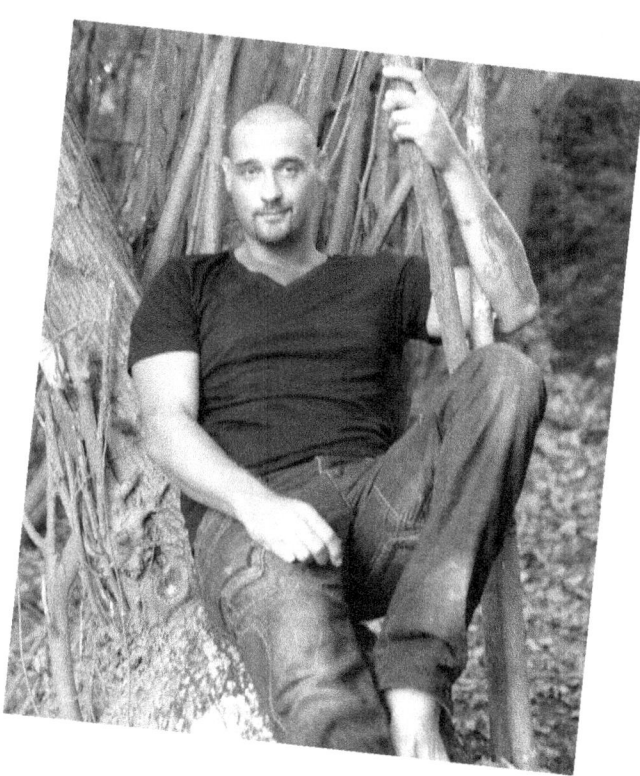

Photos above taken at Redcliffe - Photos below taken at
Benowa on the Gold Coast

page 7

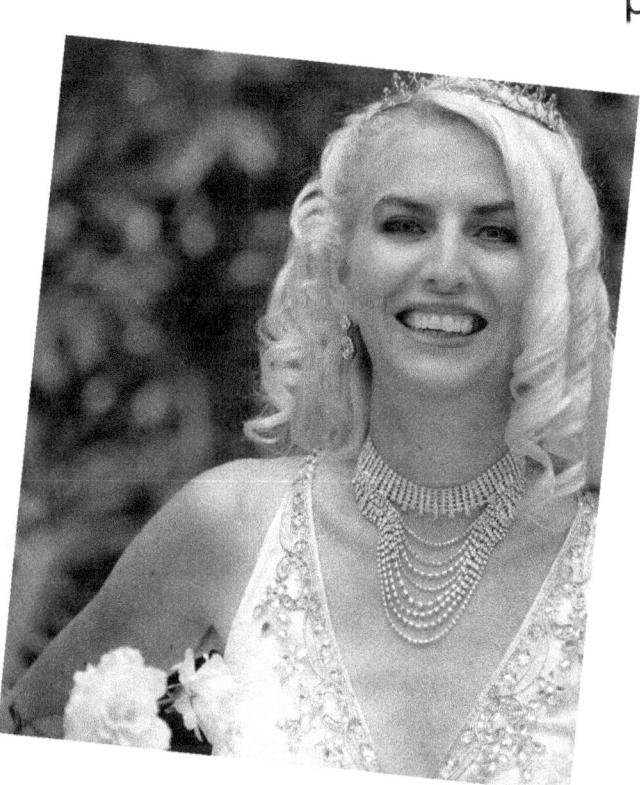 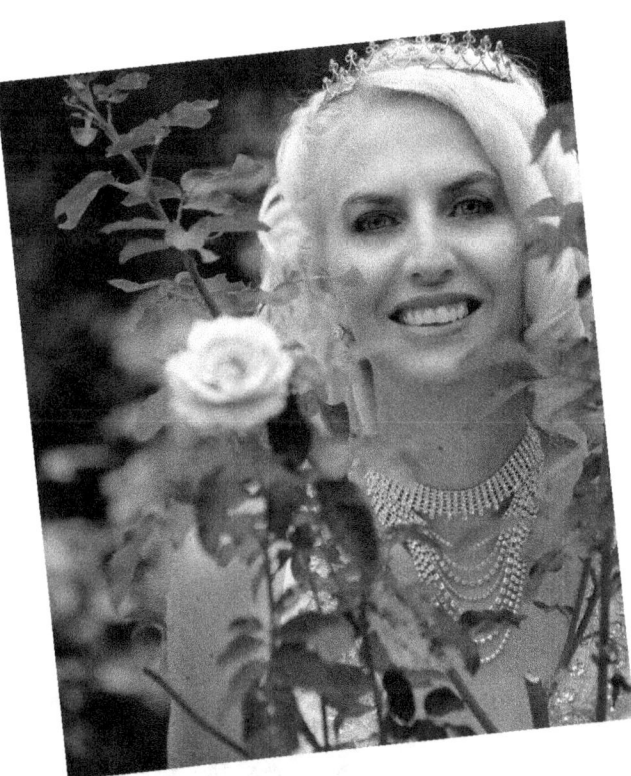

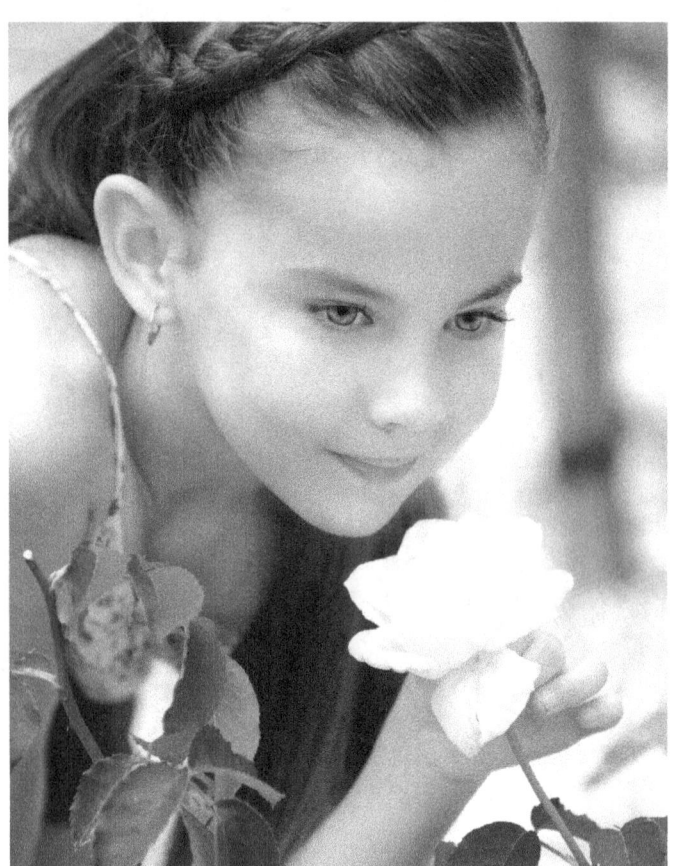
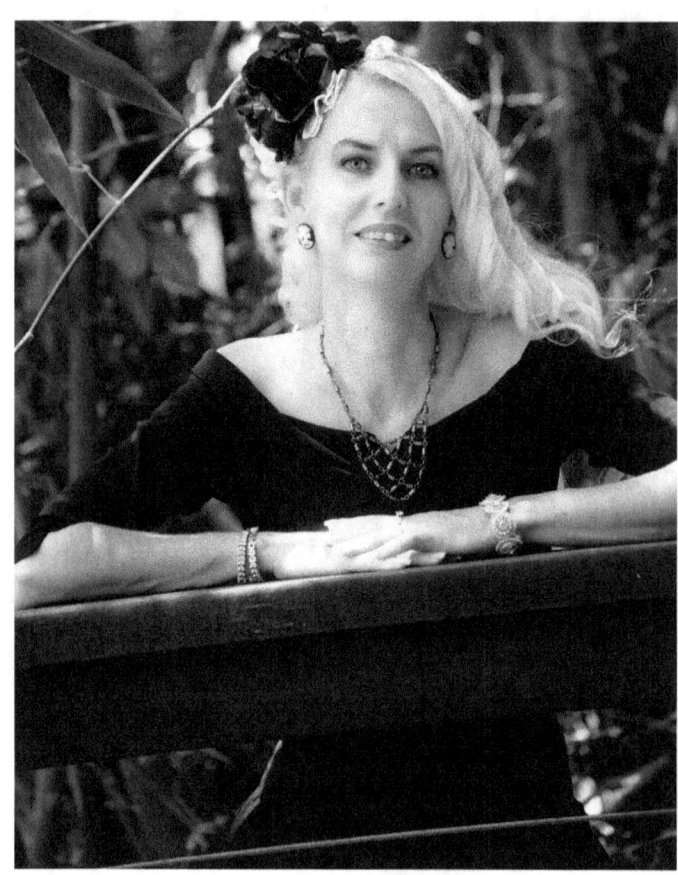

Photos above Benowa - Photos below Calamvale
page8

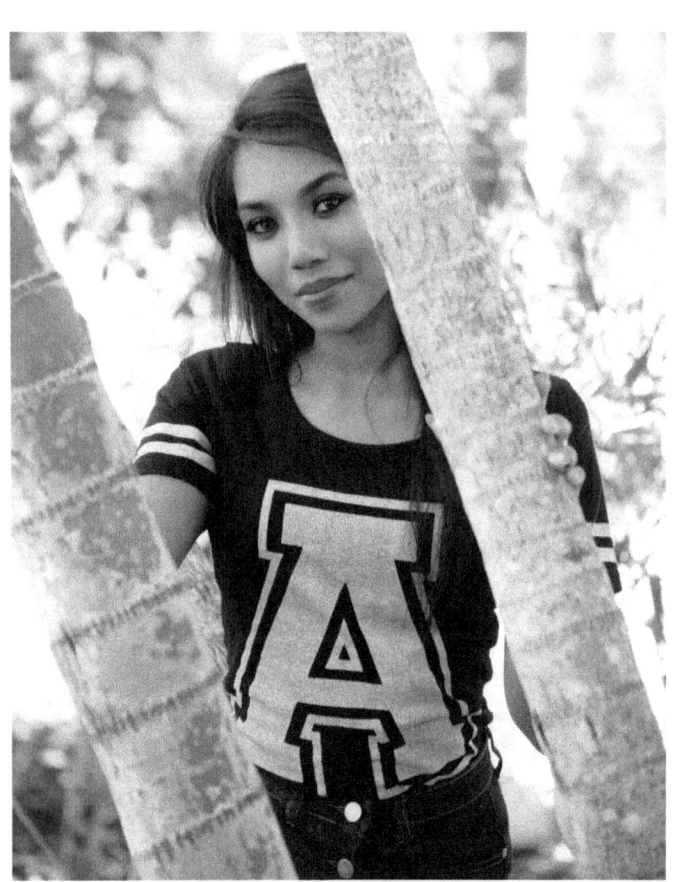
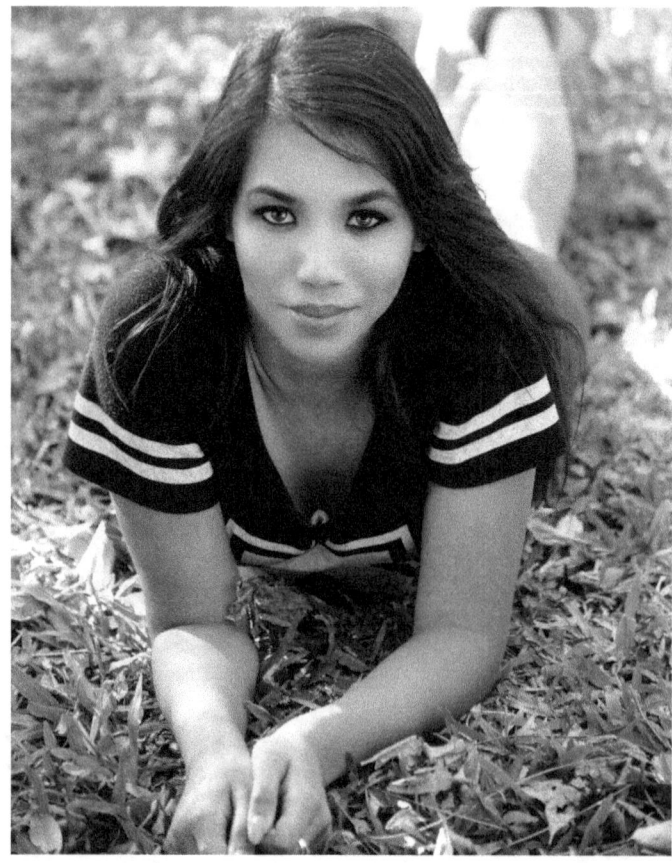

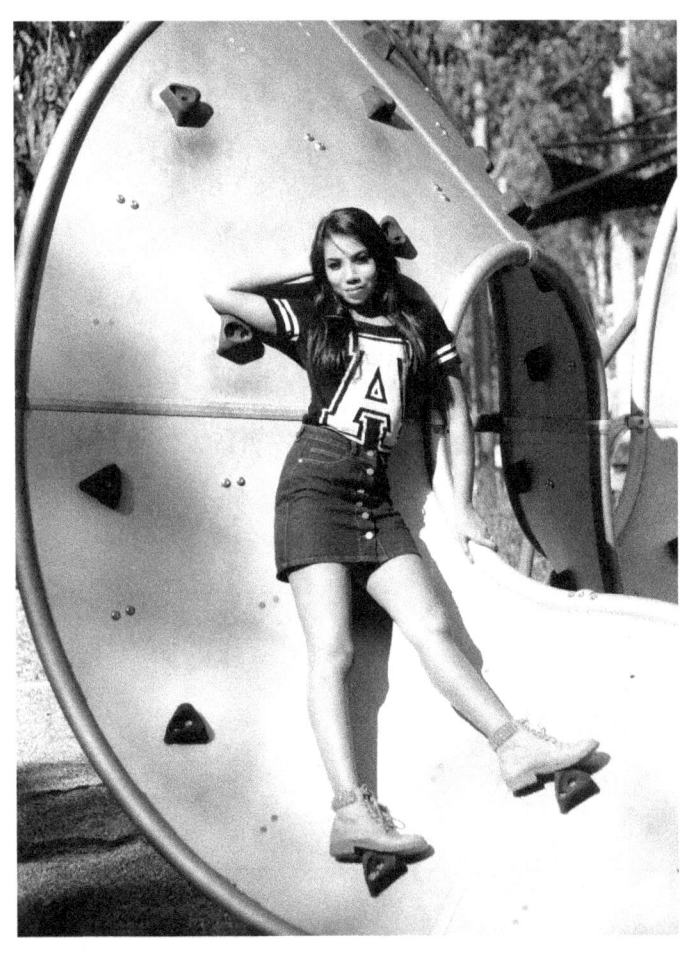
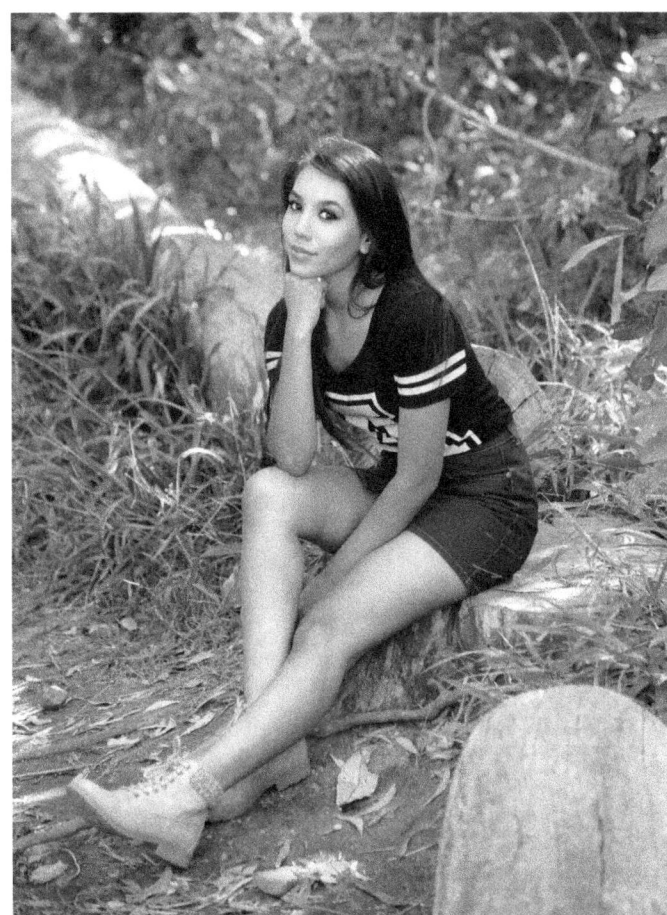
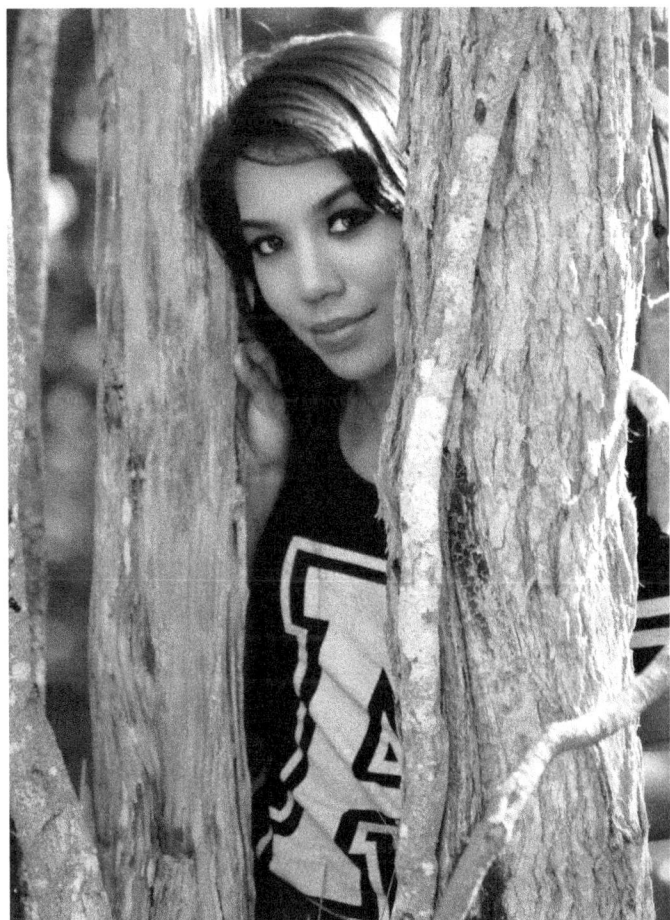
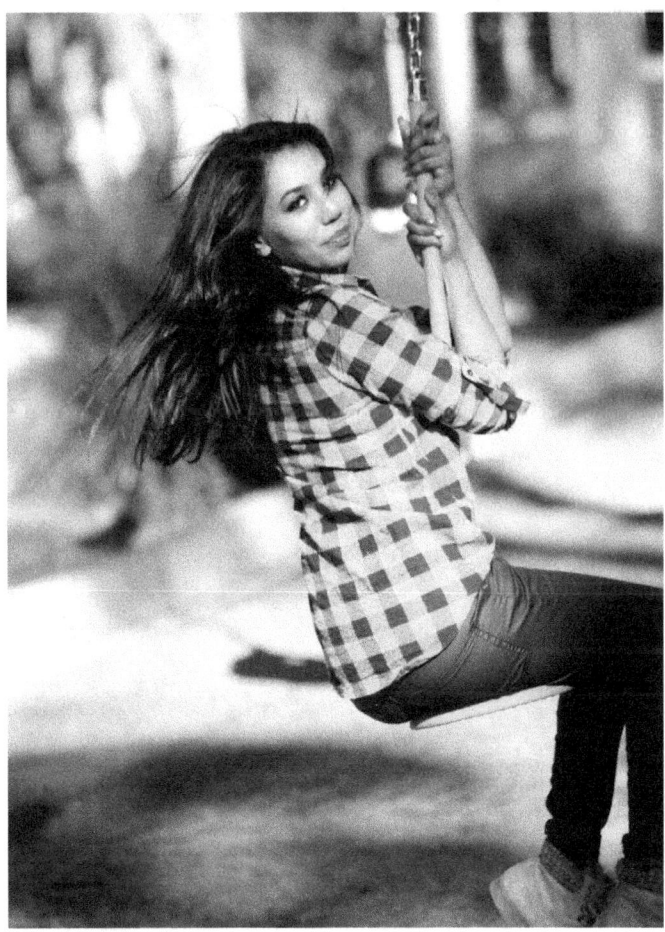

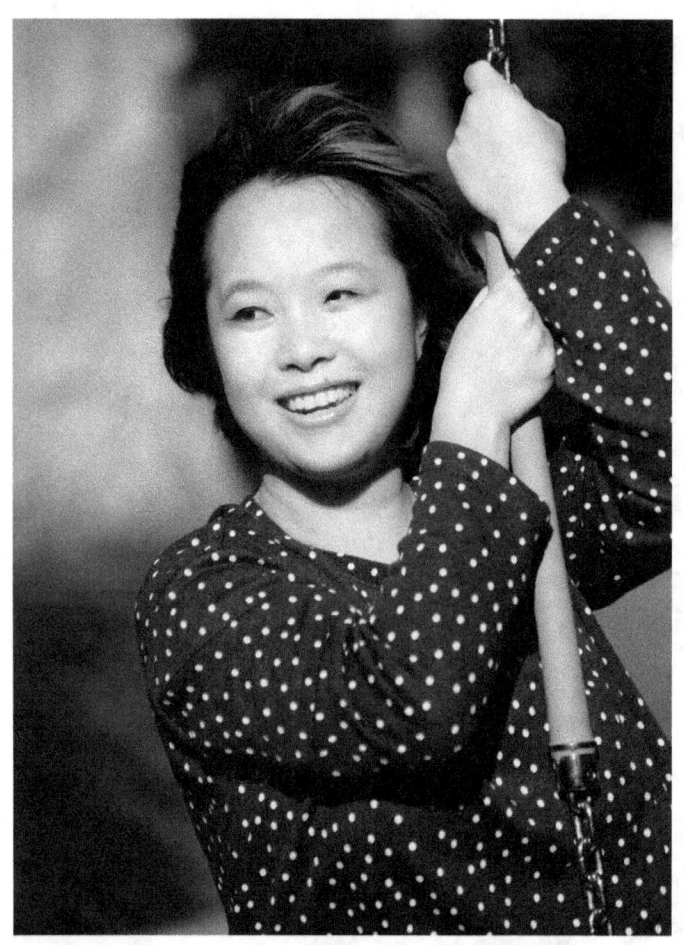

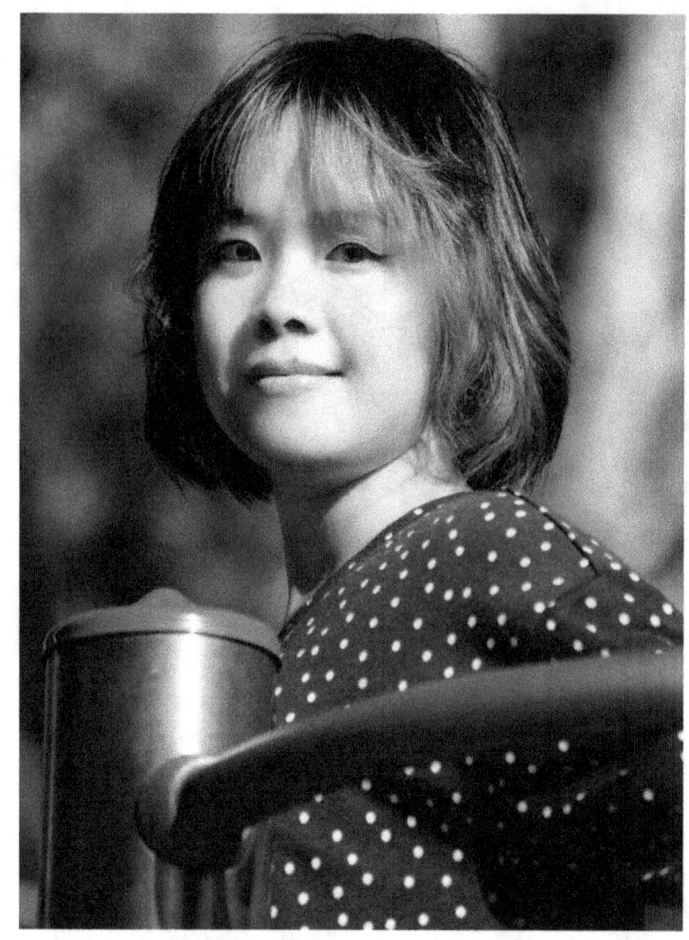

Calamvale District Park

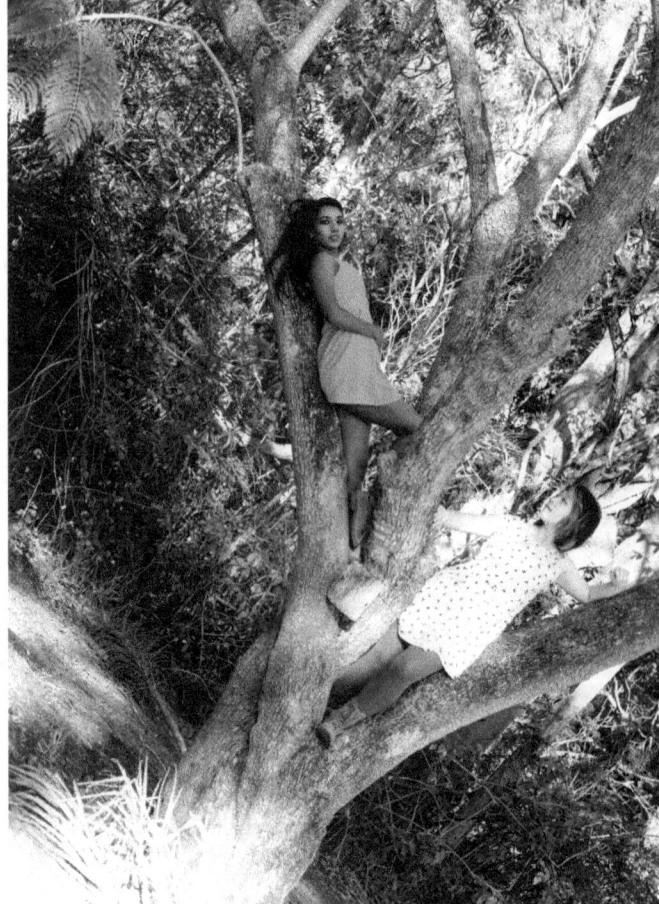

page 10

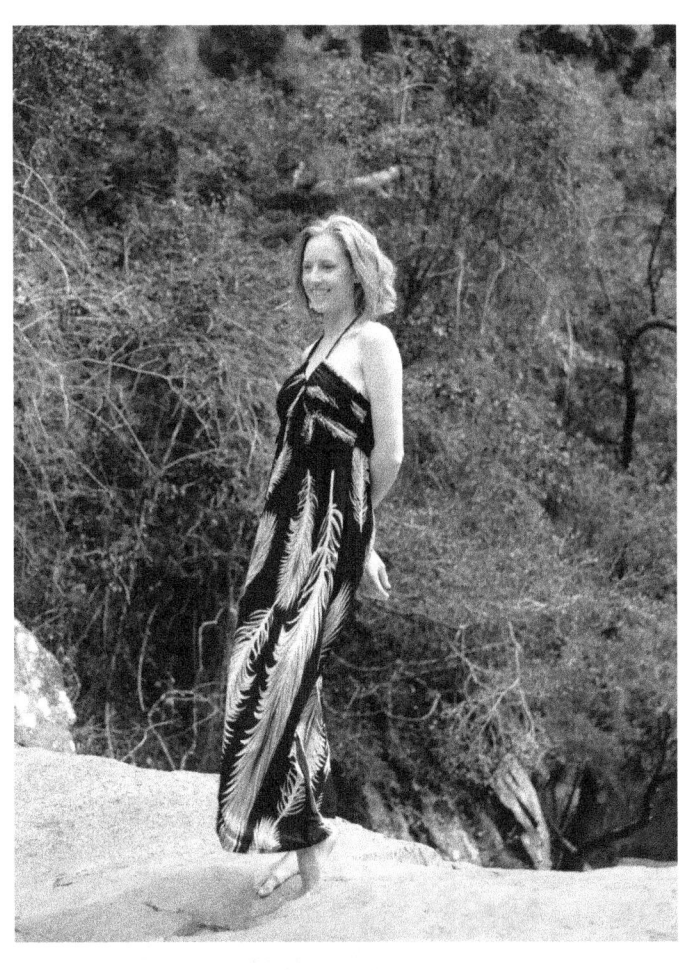
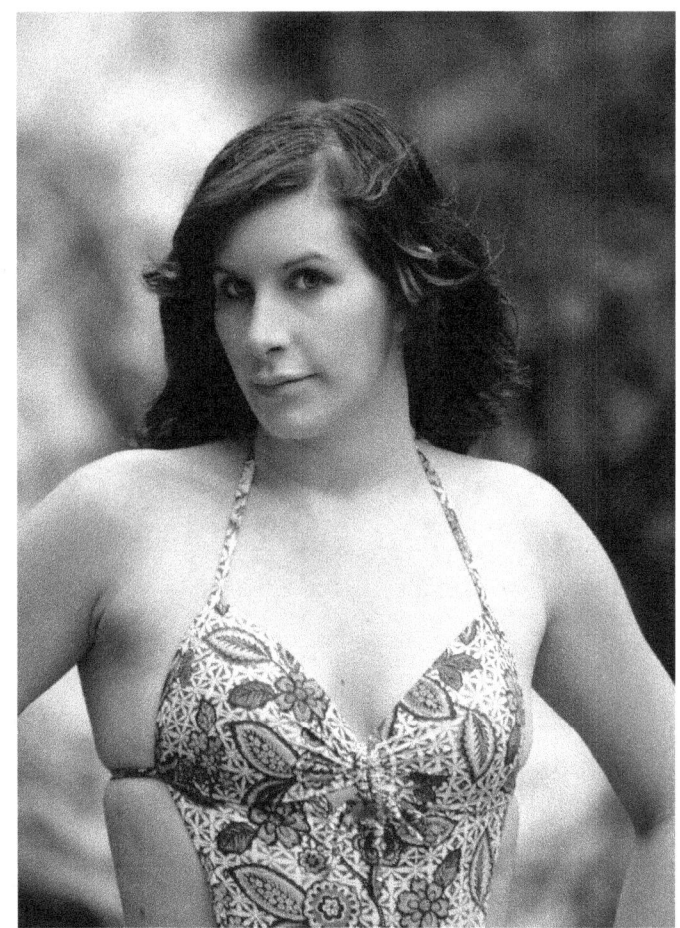
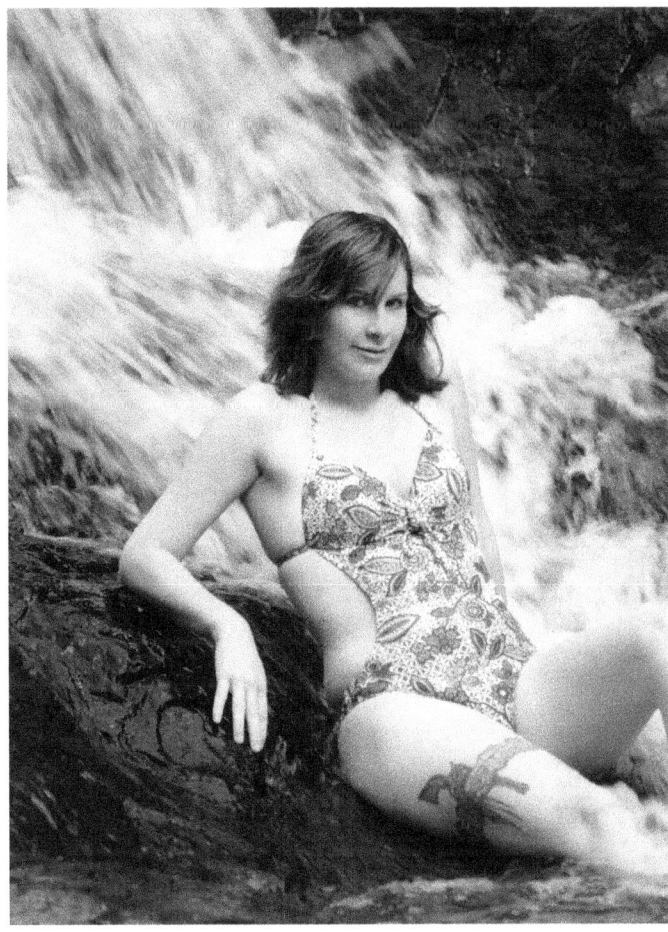
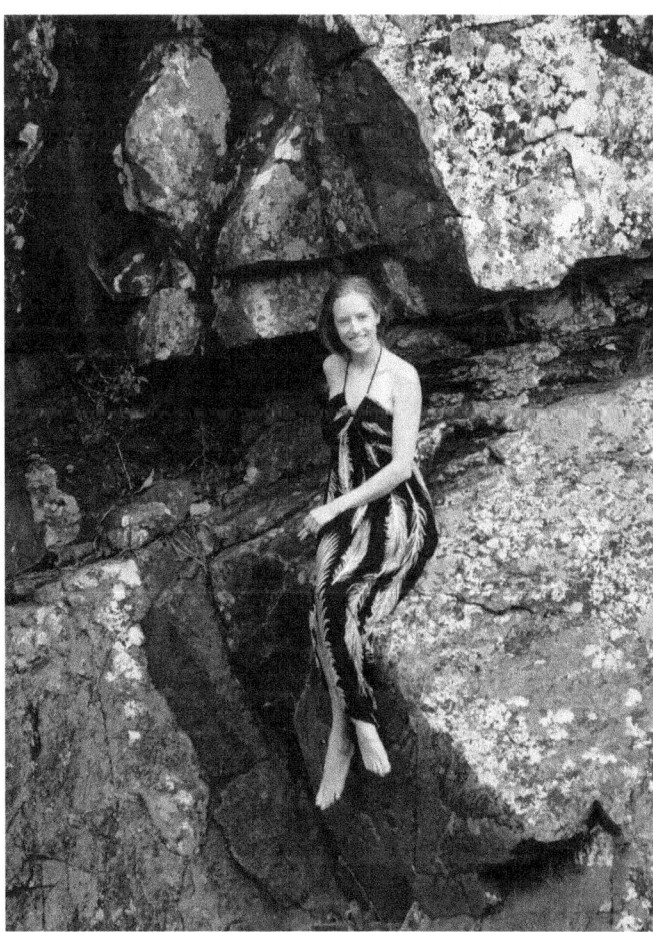

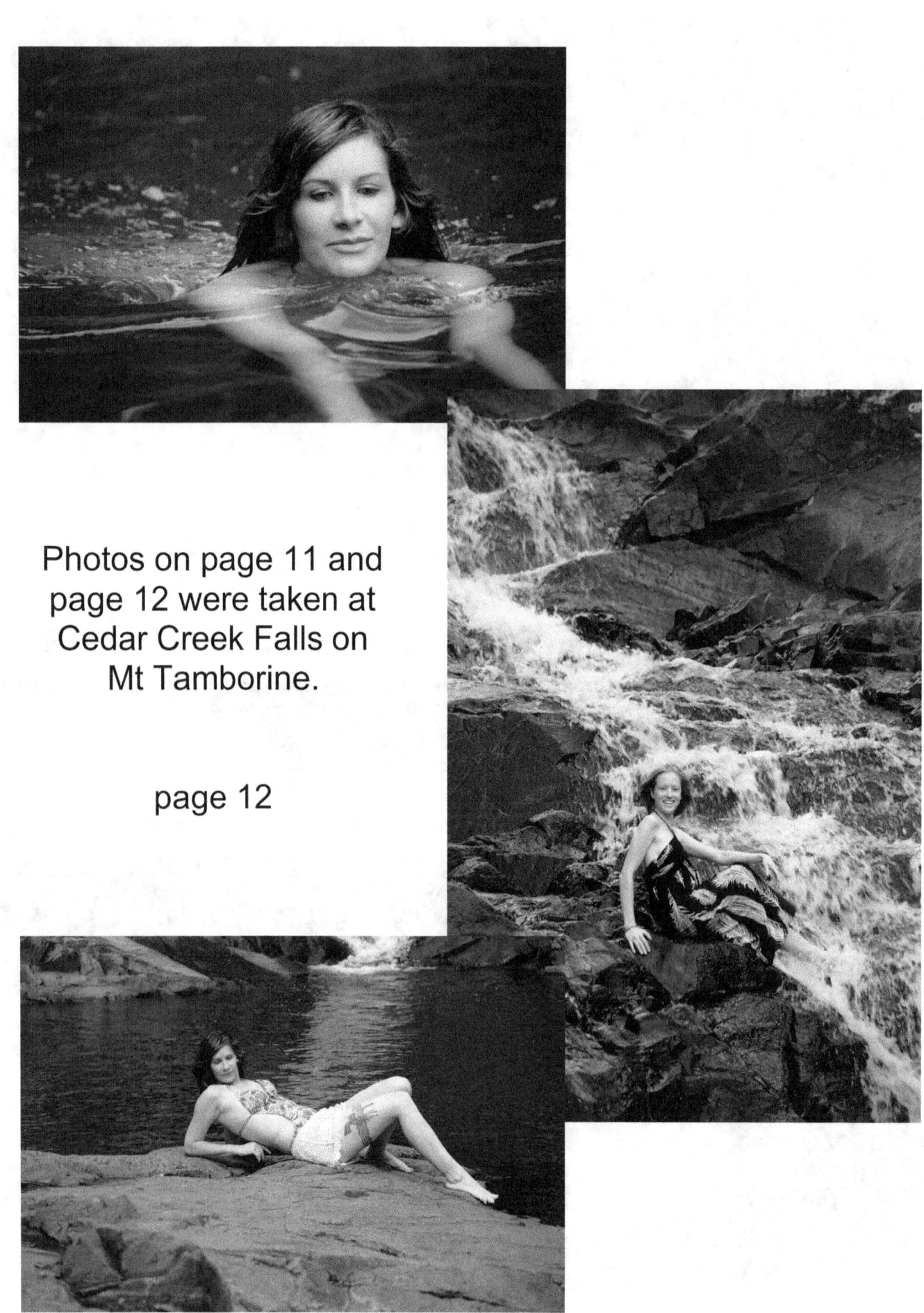

Photos on page 11 and
page 12 were taken at
Cedar Creek Falls on
Mt Tamborine.

page 12

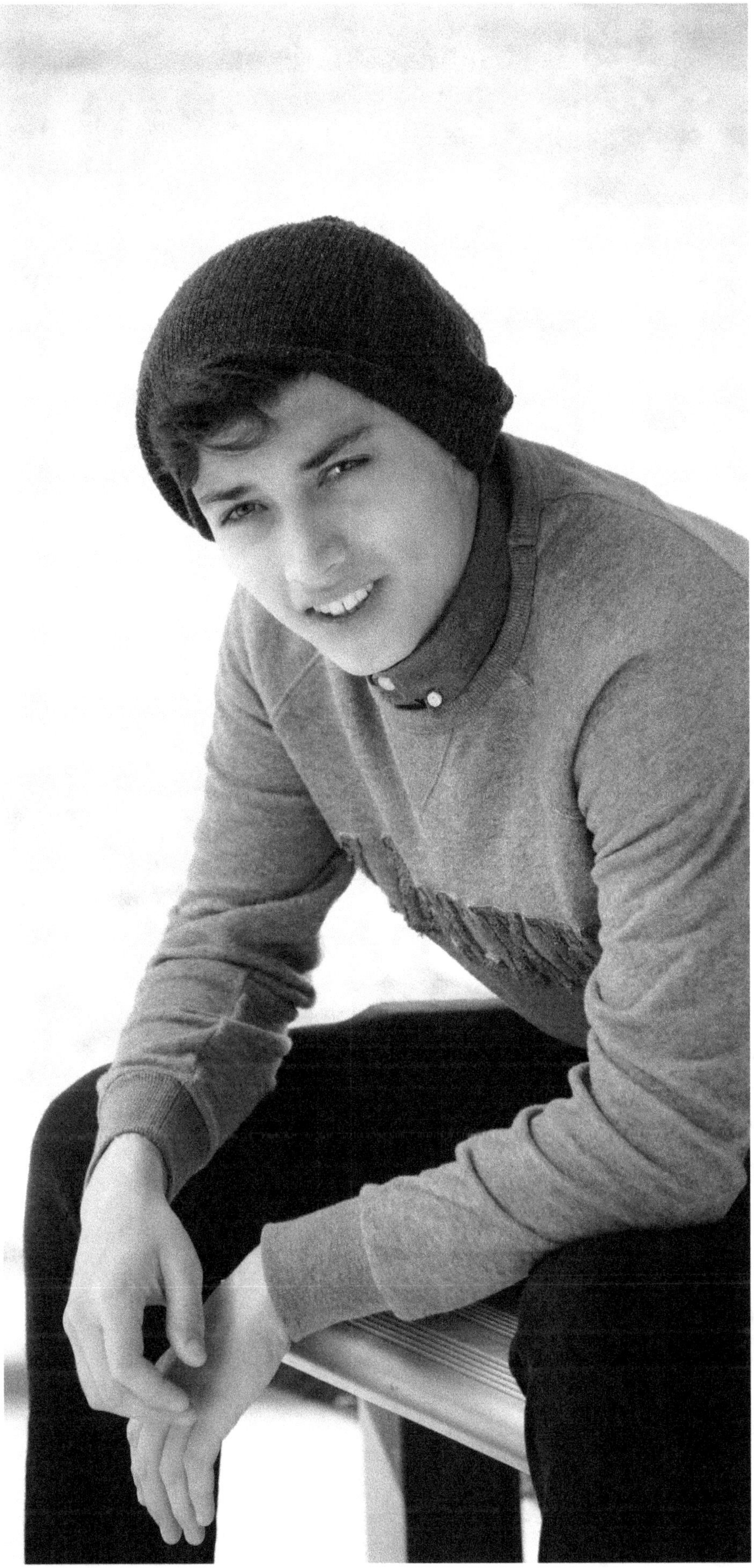

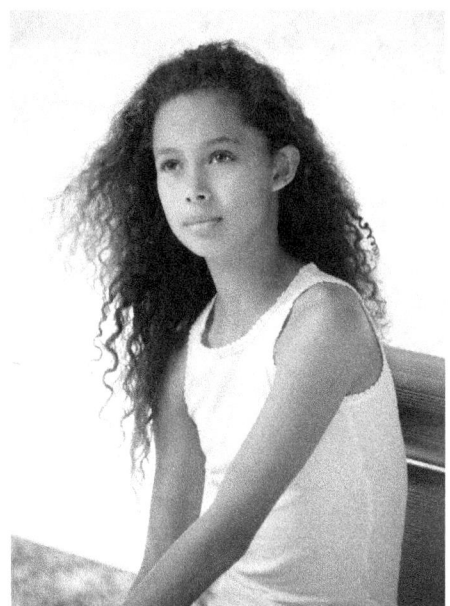

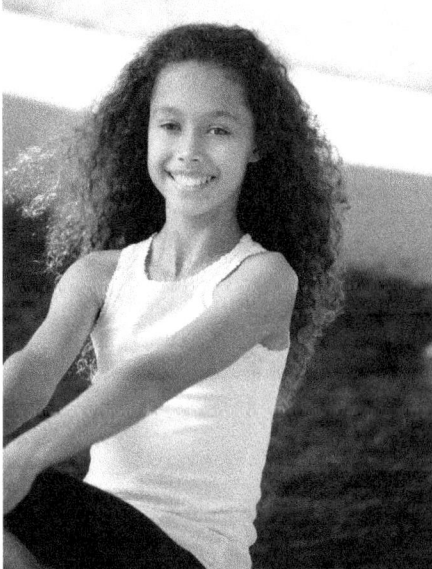

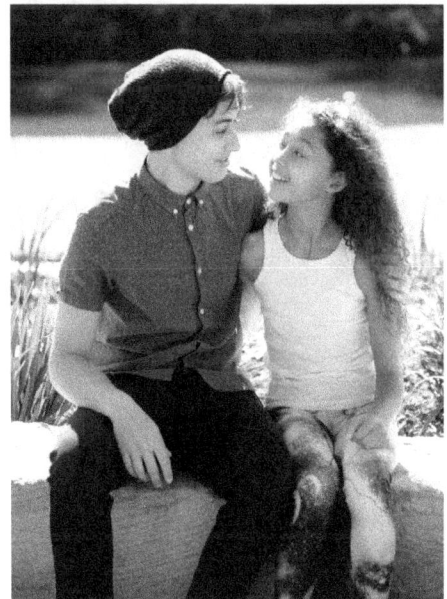

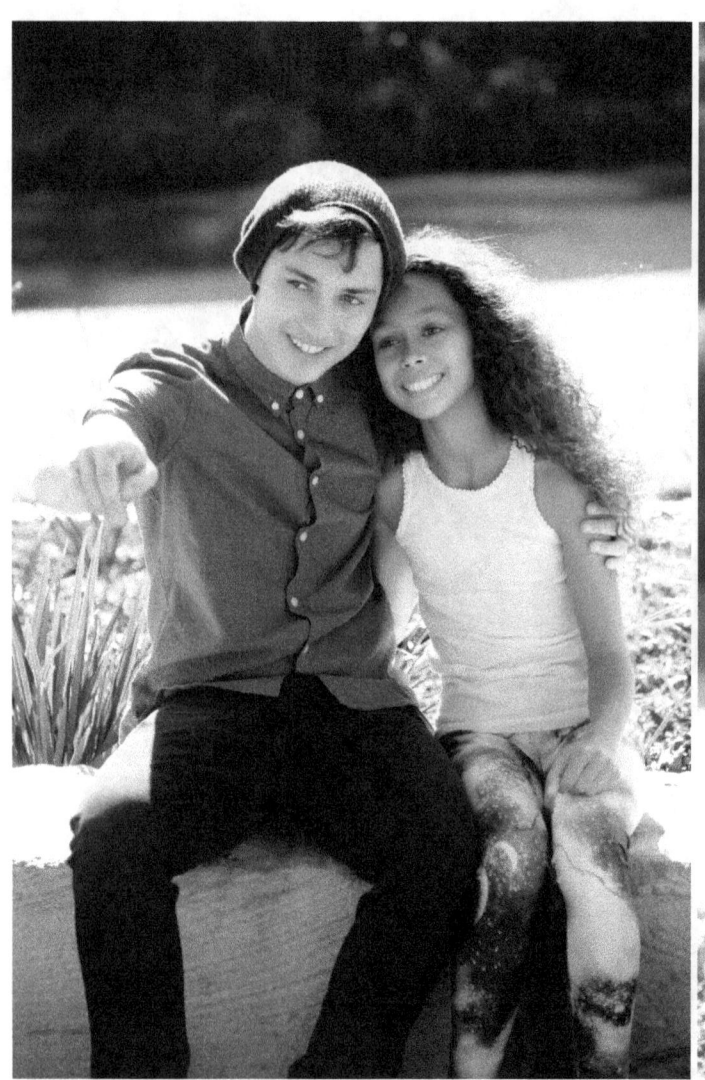

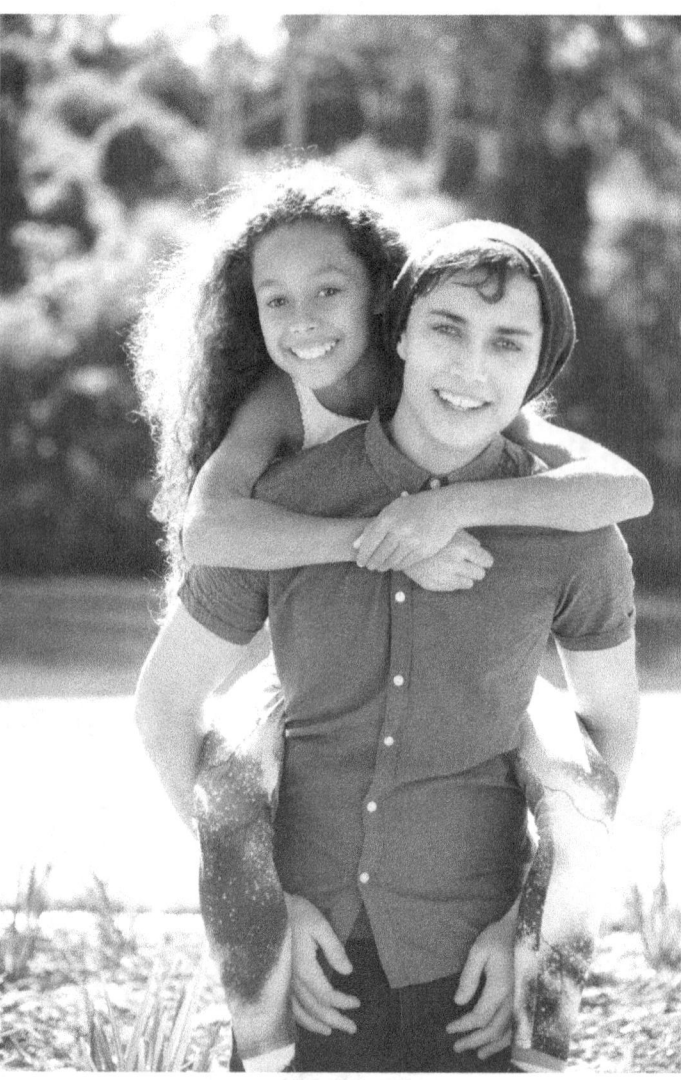

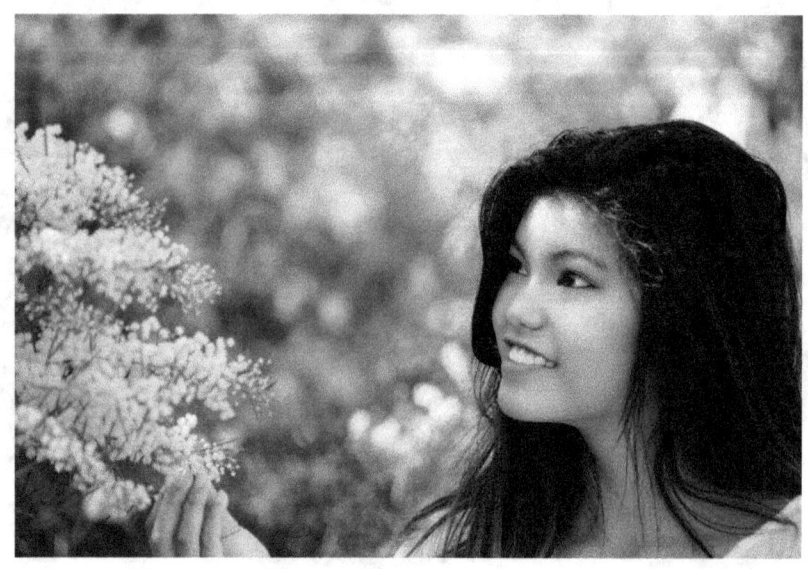

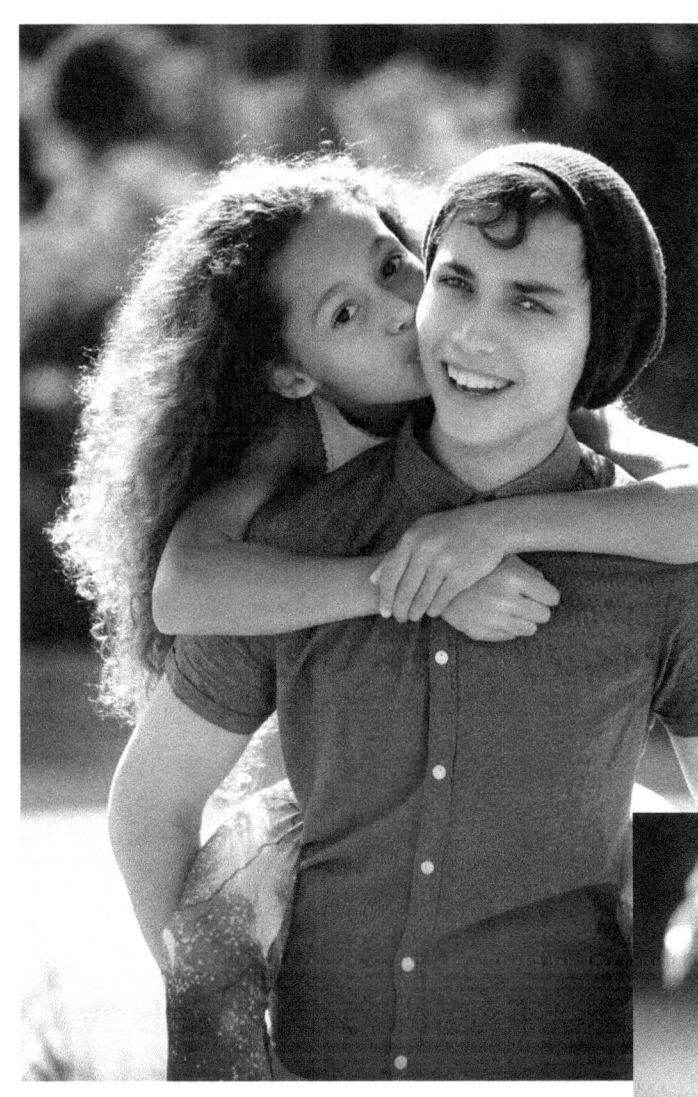

Photos on pages 13, 14 and 15 were taken at Colleges Crossing

page 15

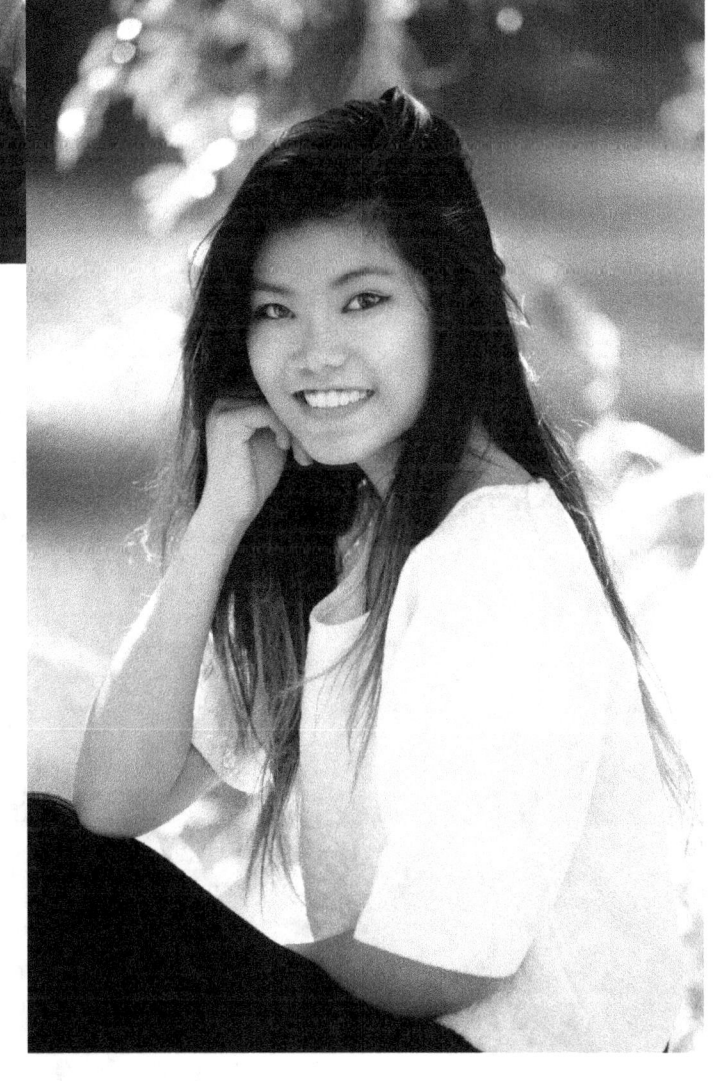

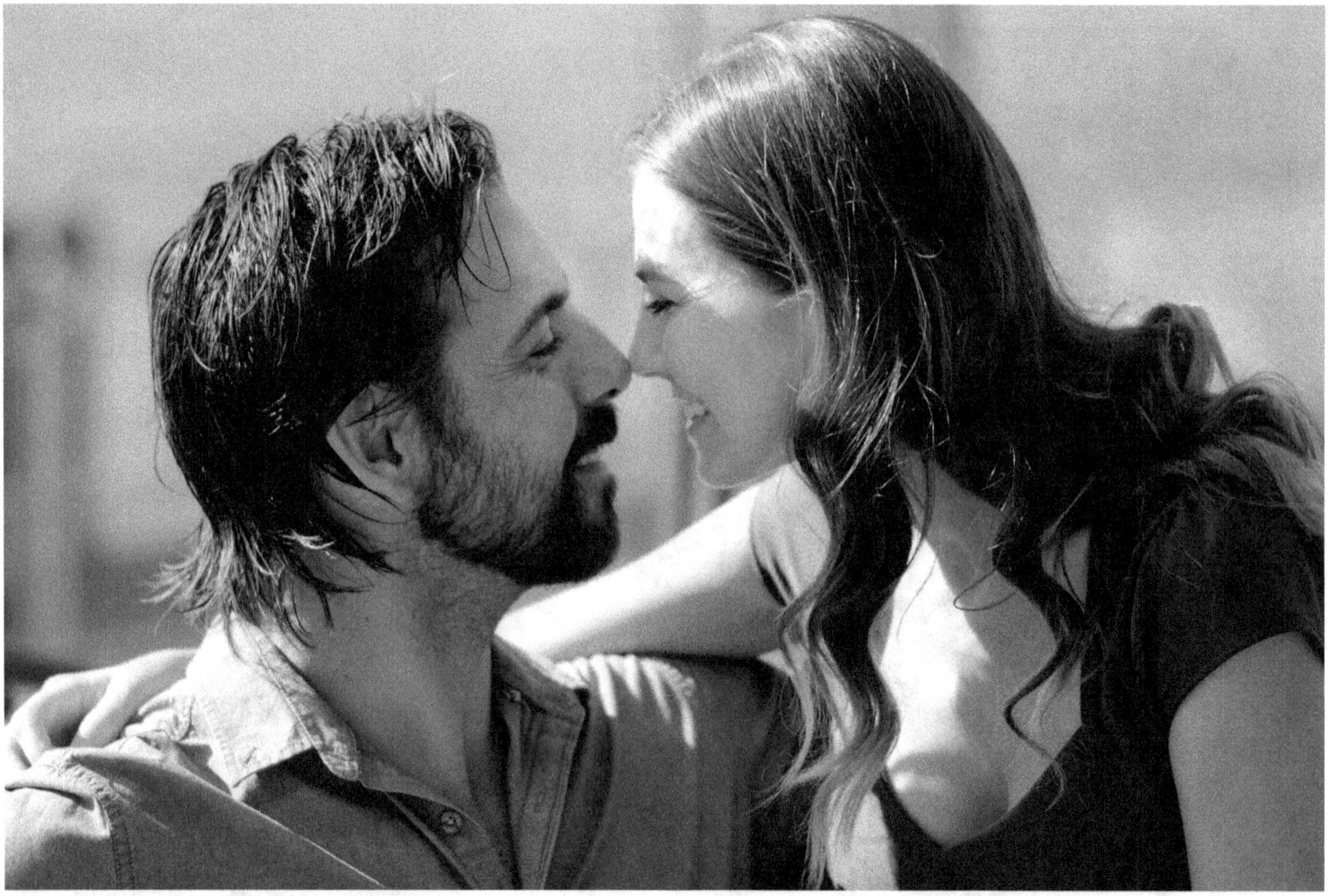

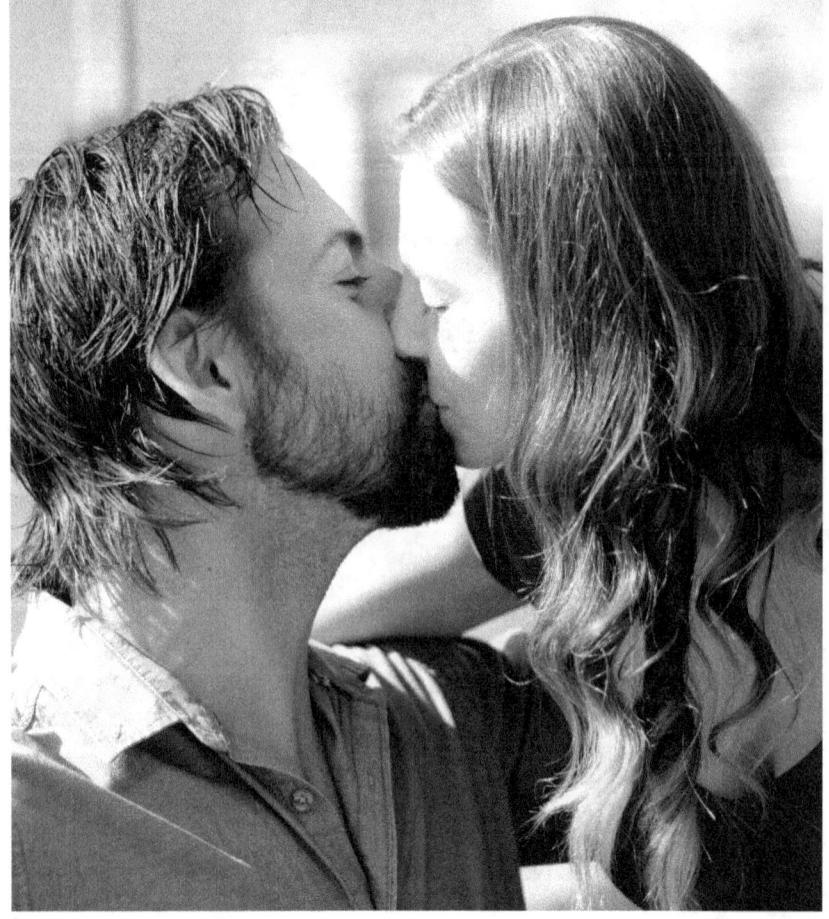

Valentines Day
couples shoot at
Brisbane Riverside

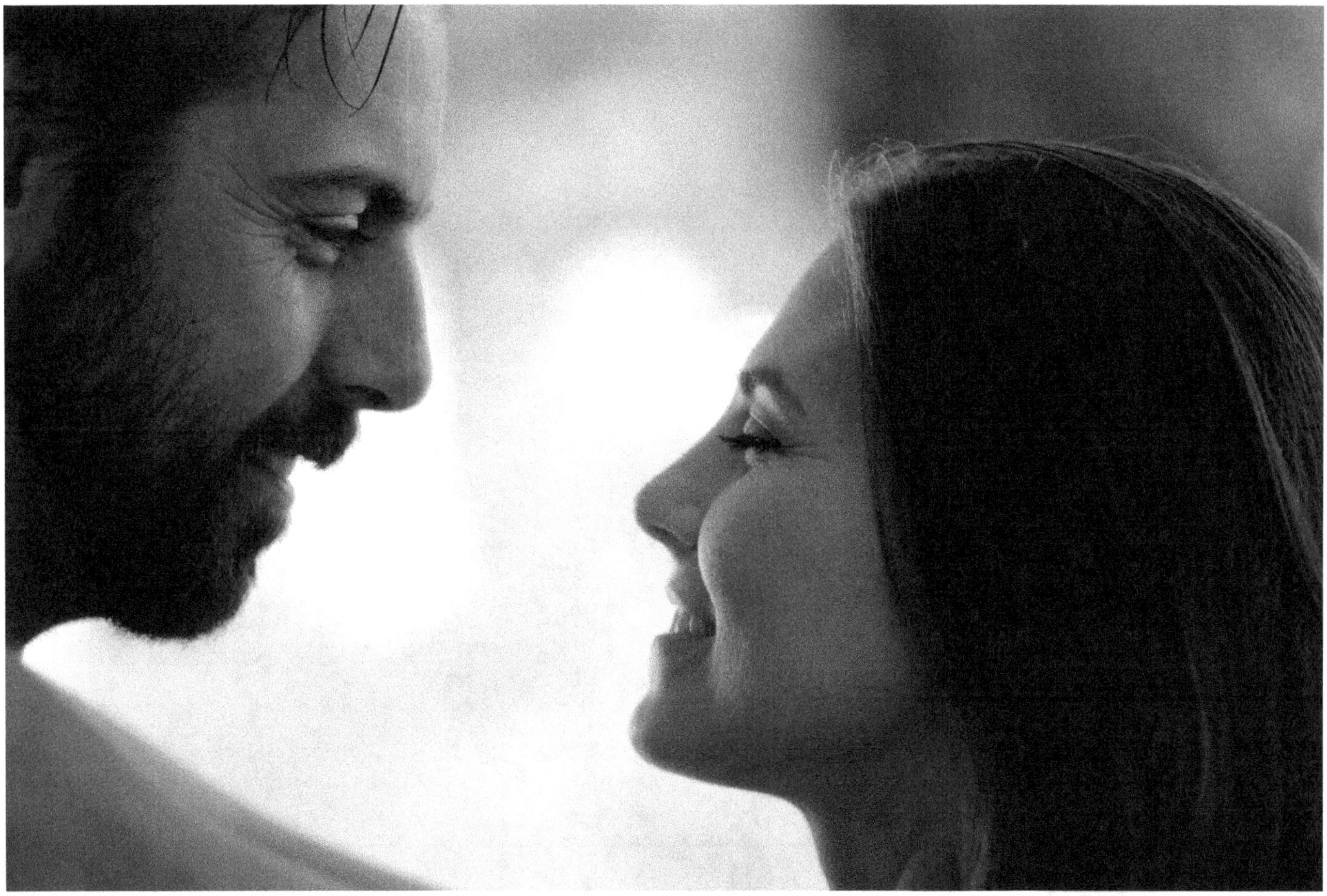

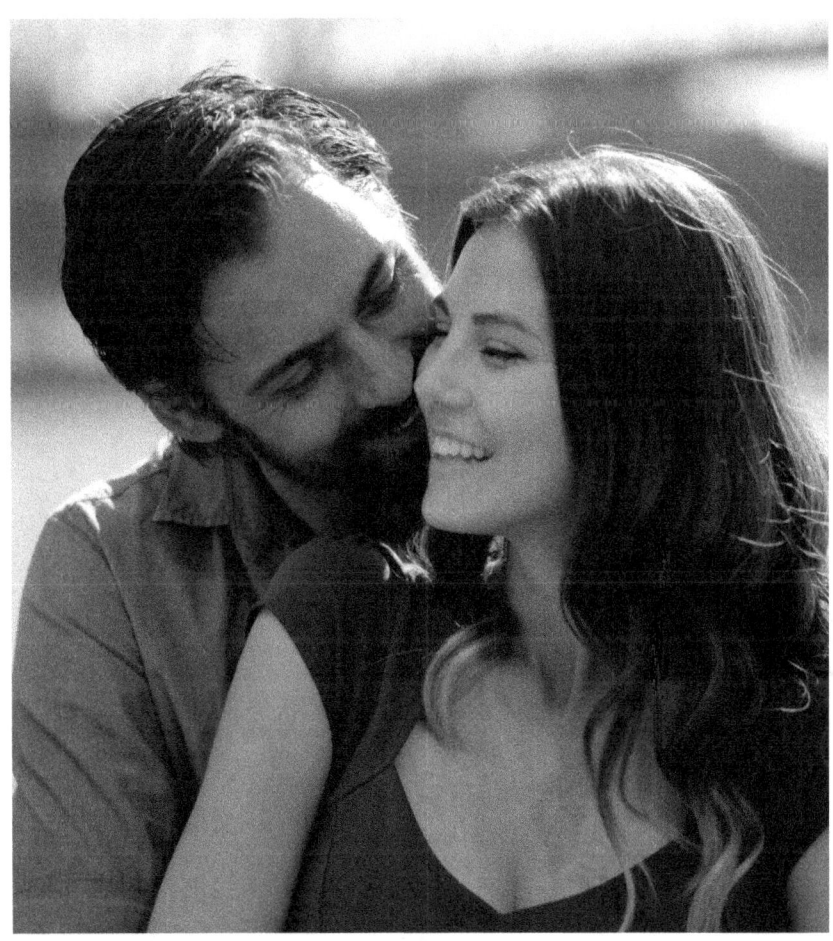

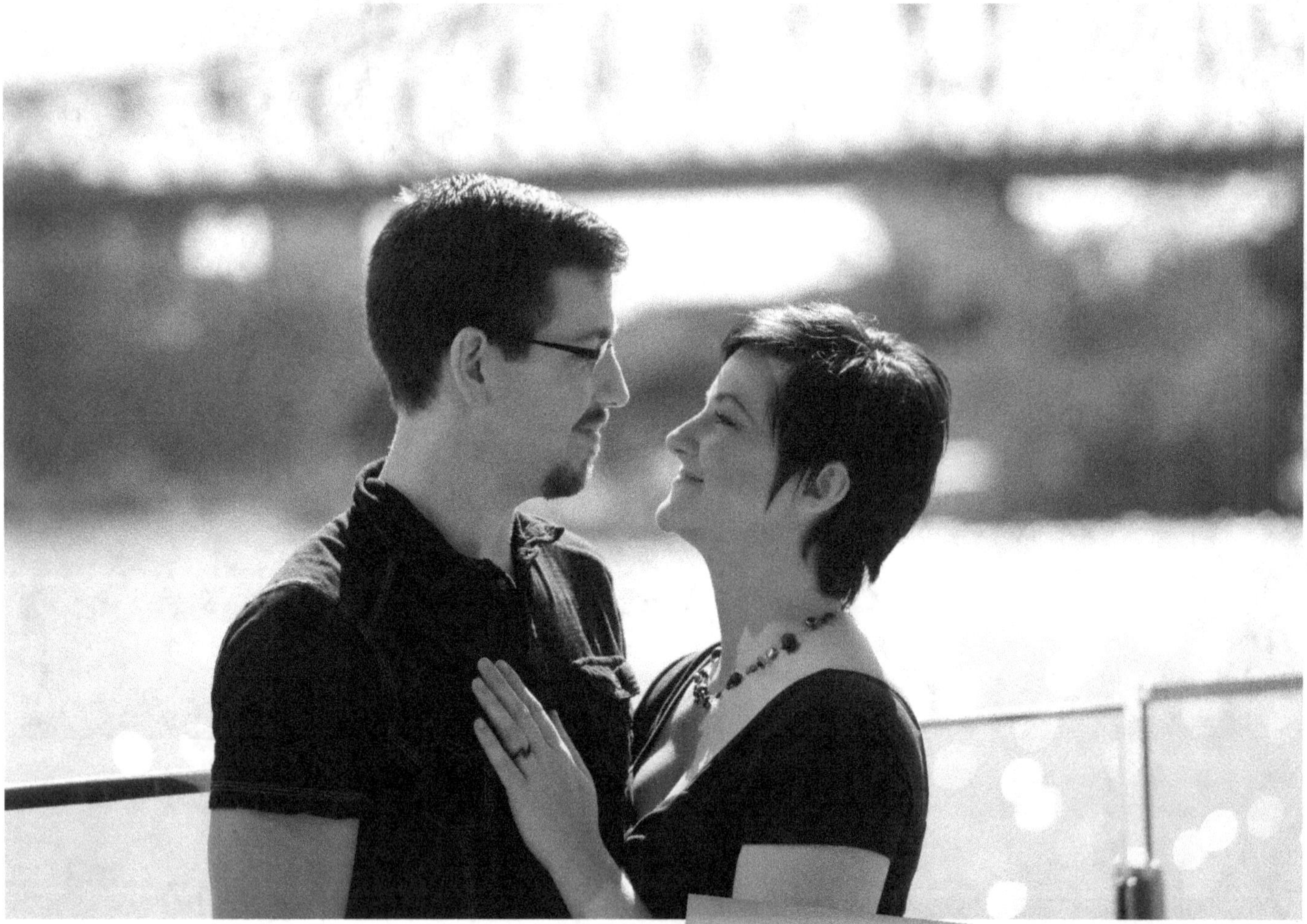

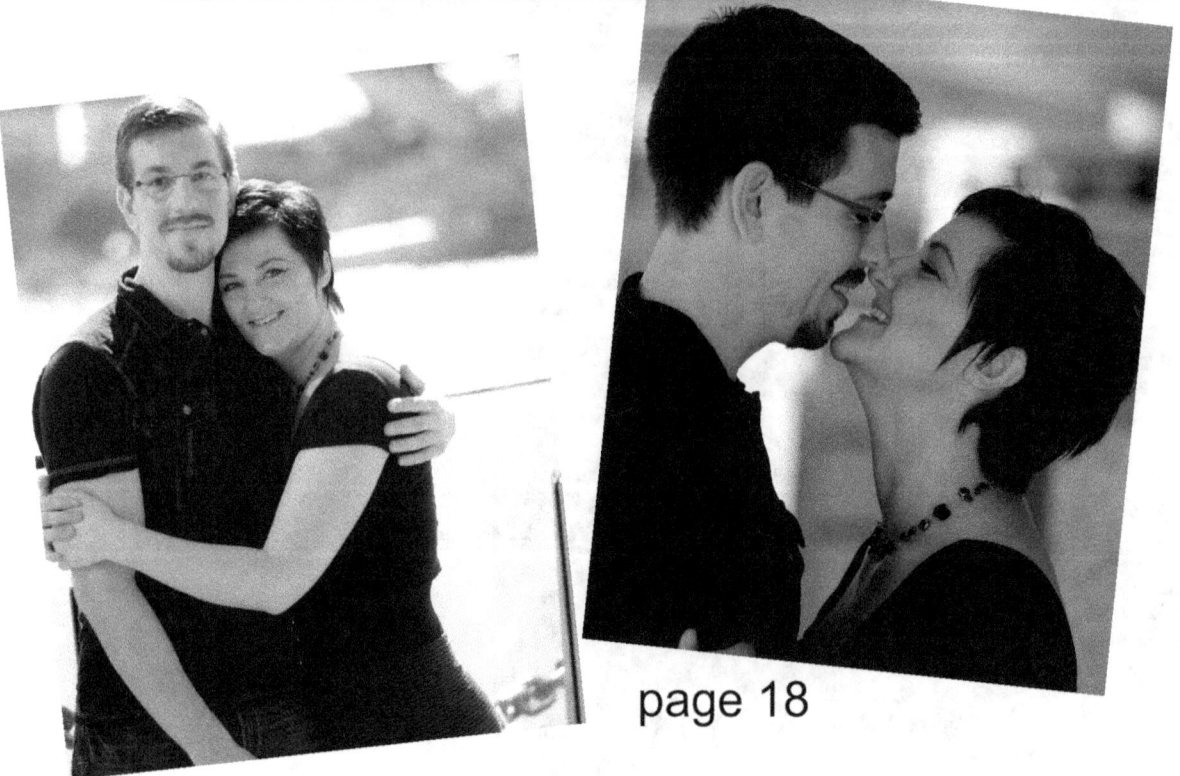

page 18

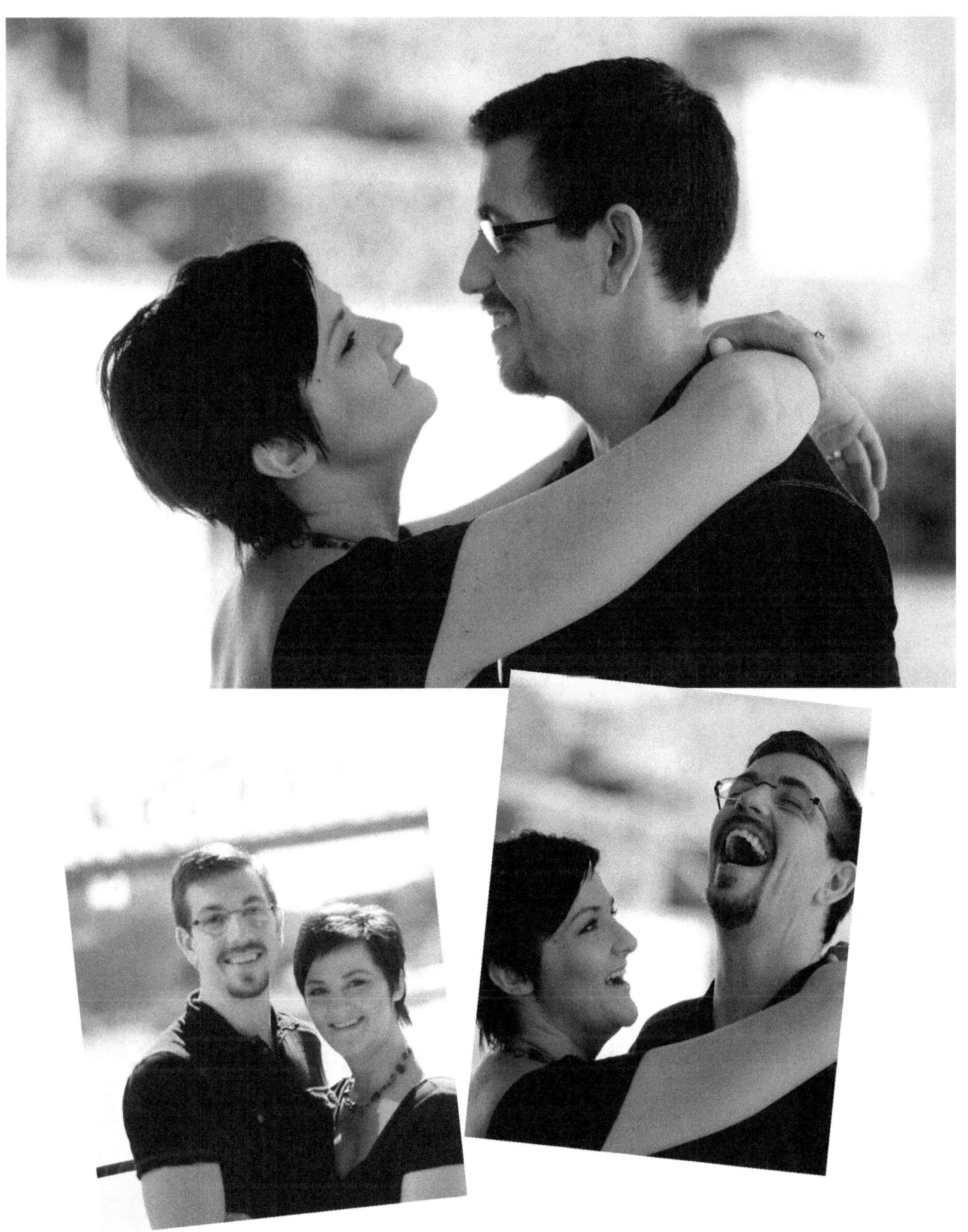

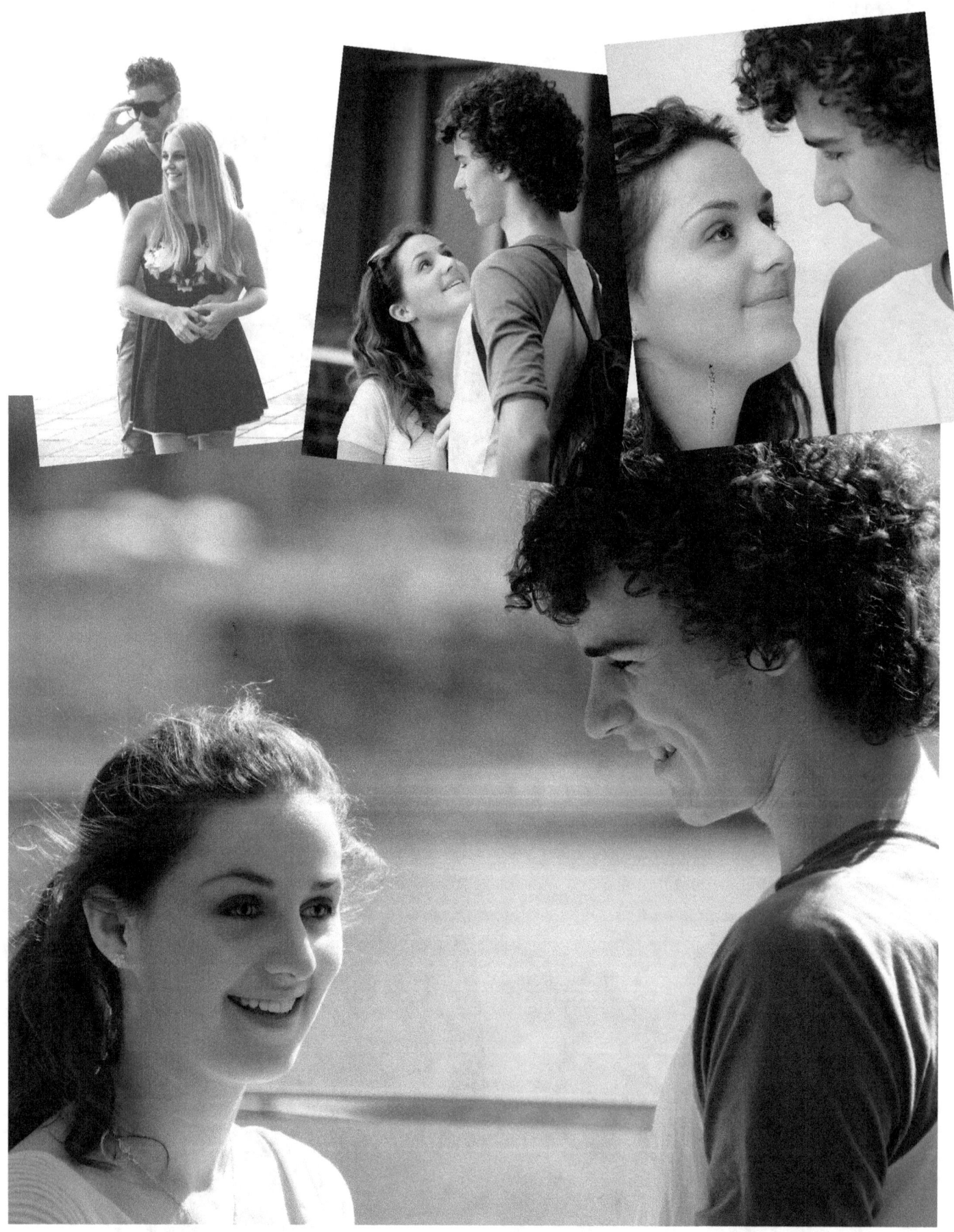

page 20

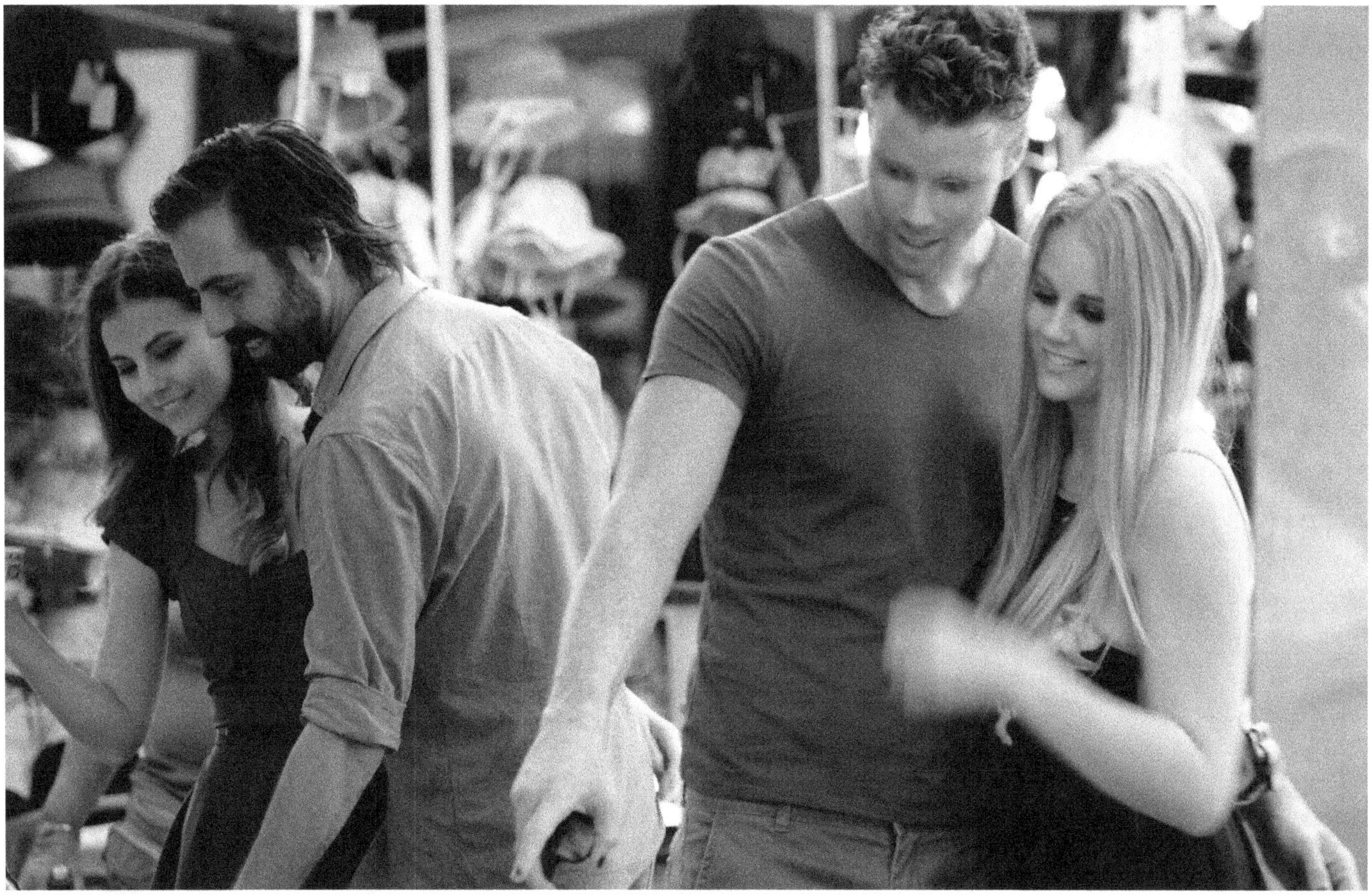

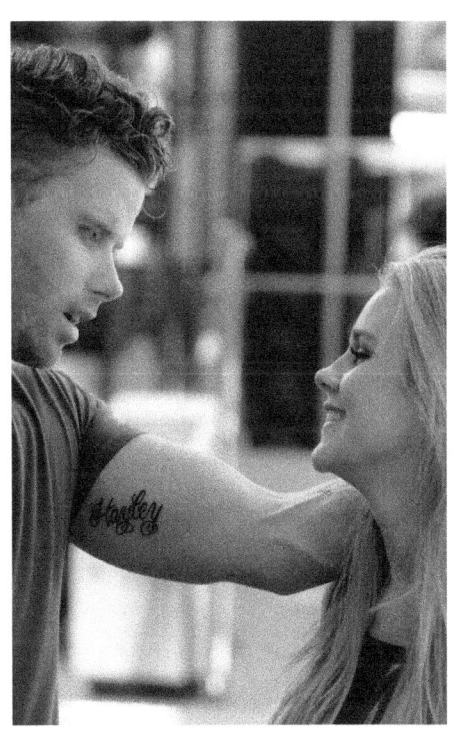

page 21

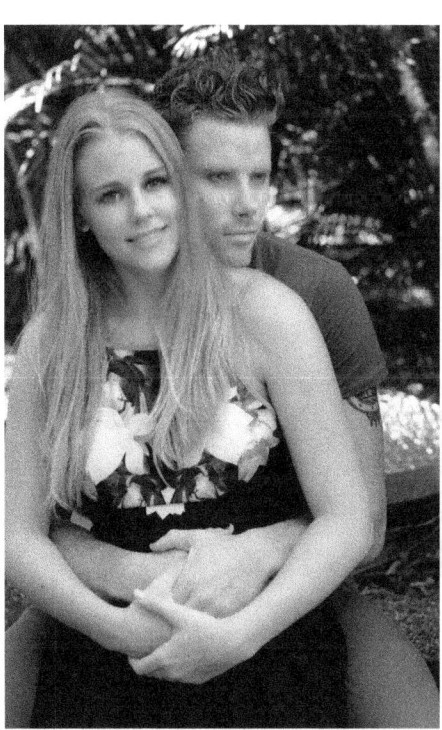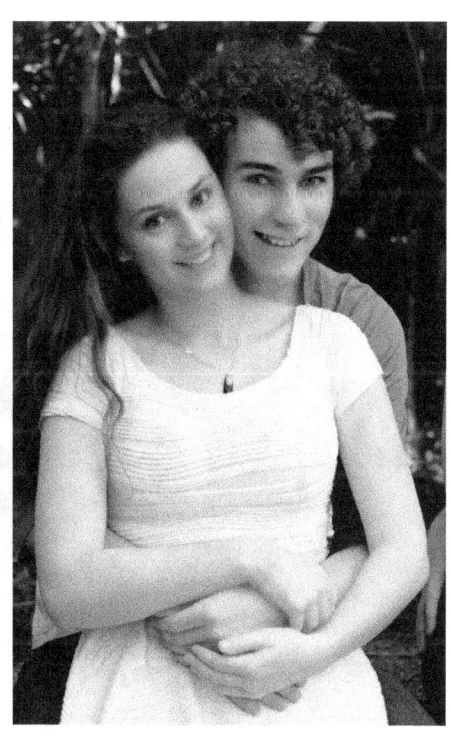

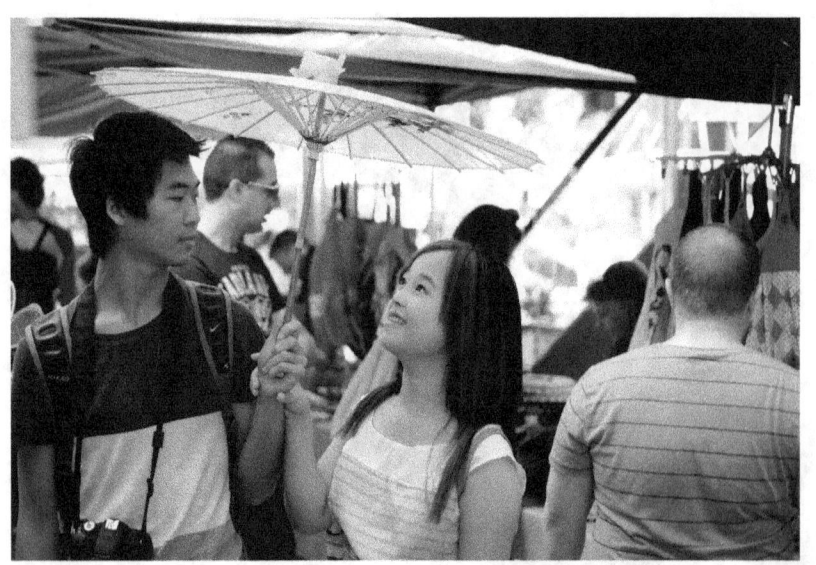

page 22

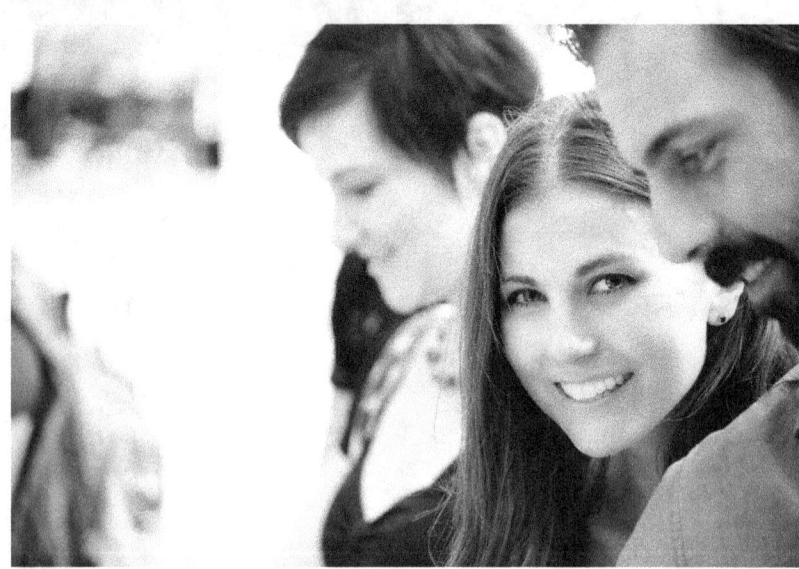

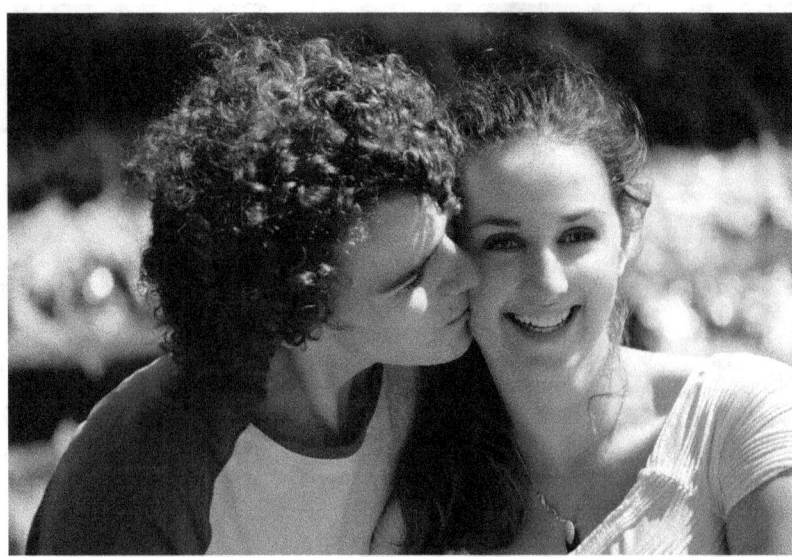

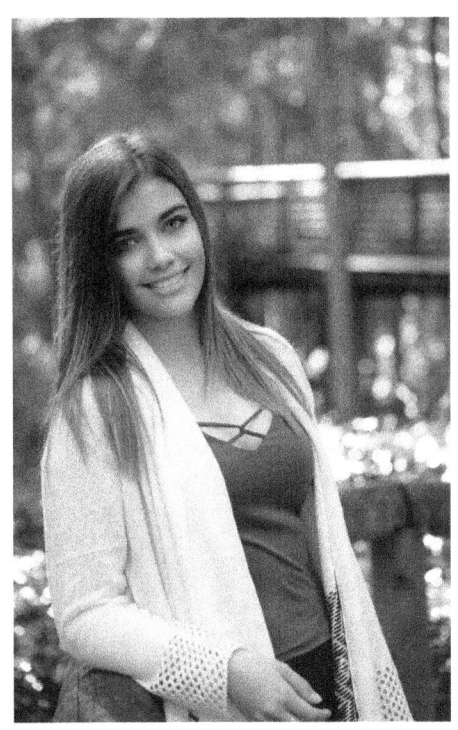 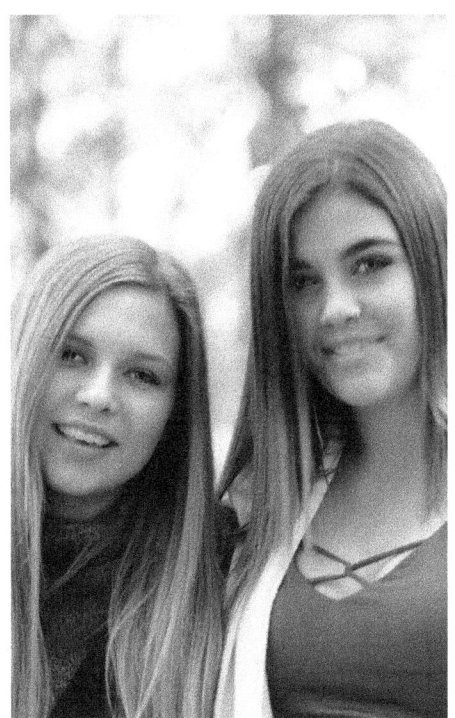 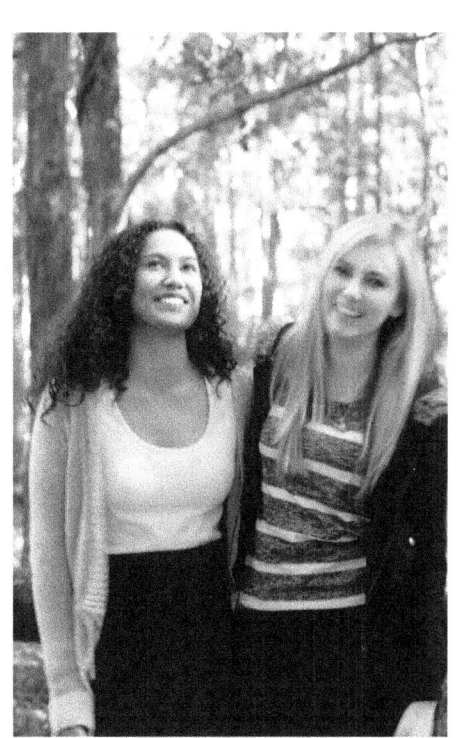

Daisy Hill

page 23

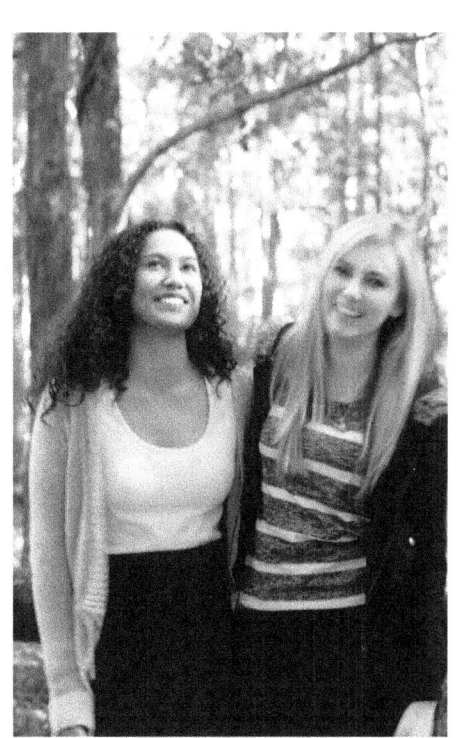

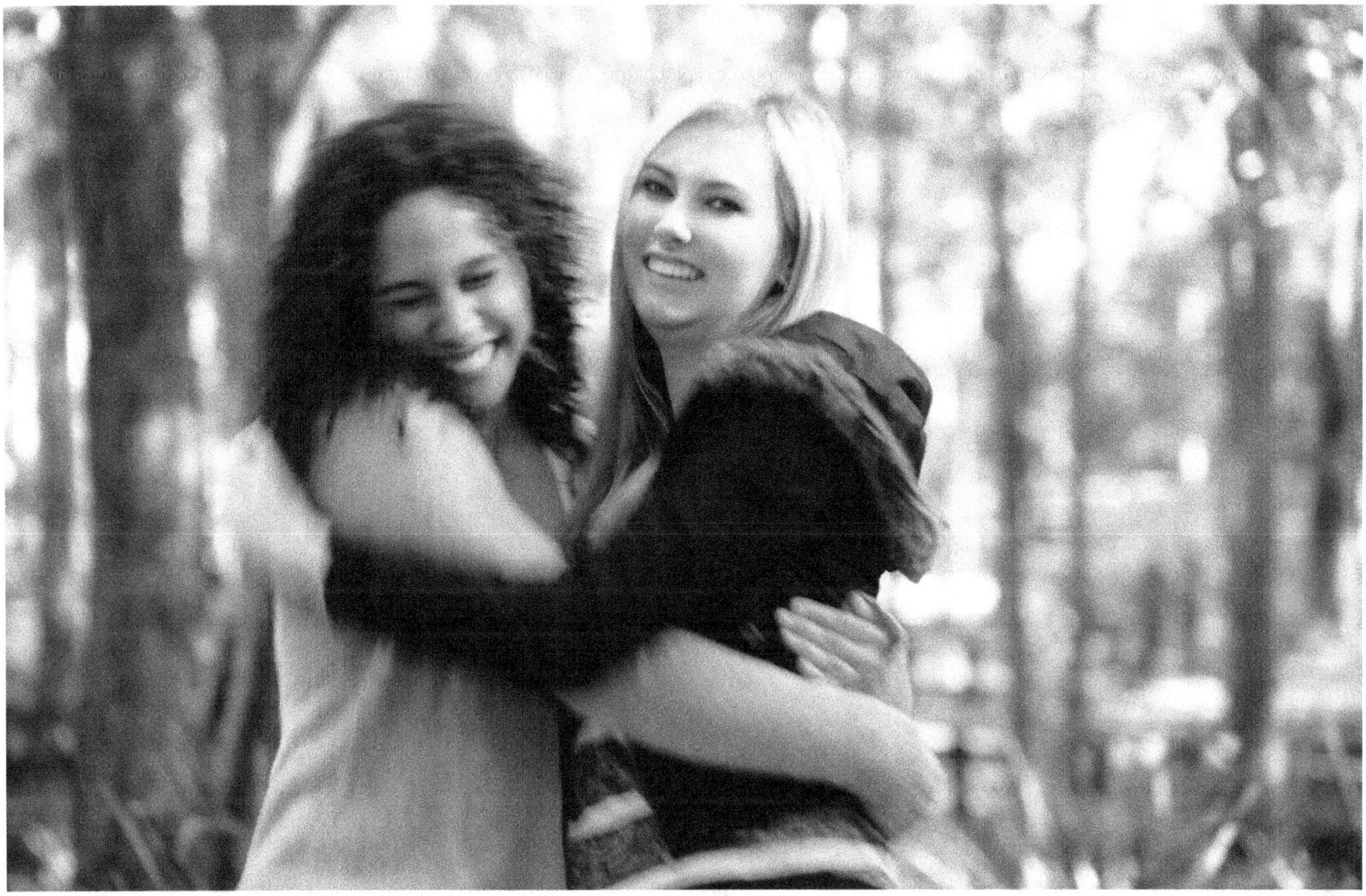

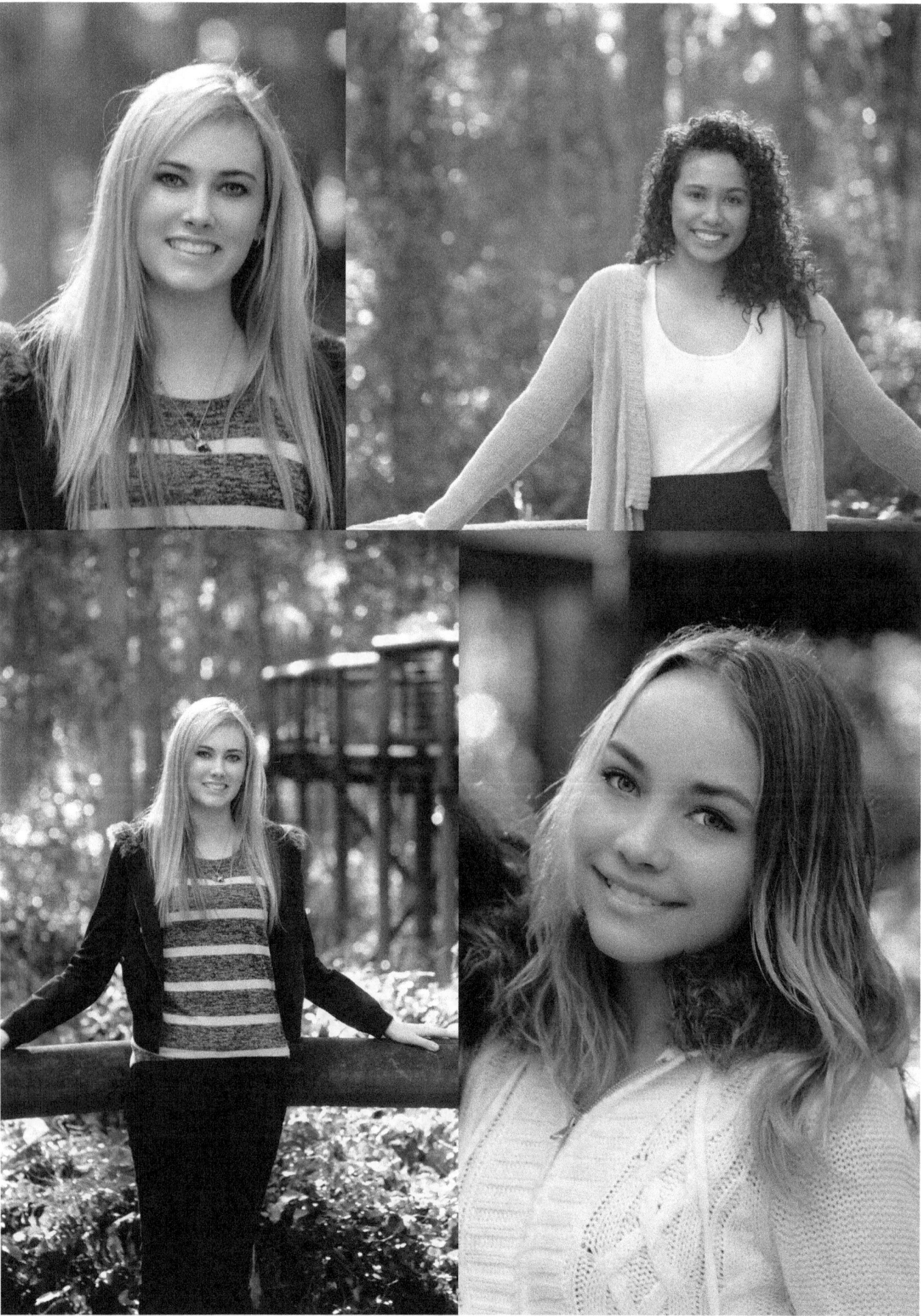

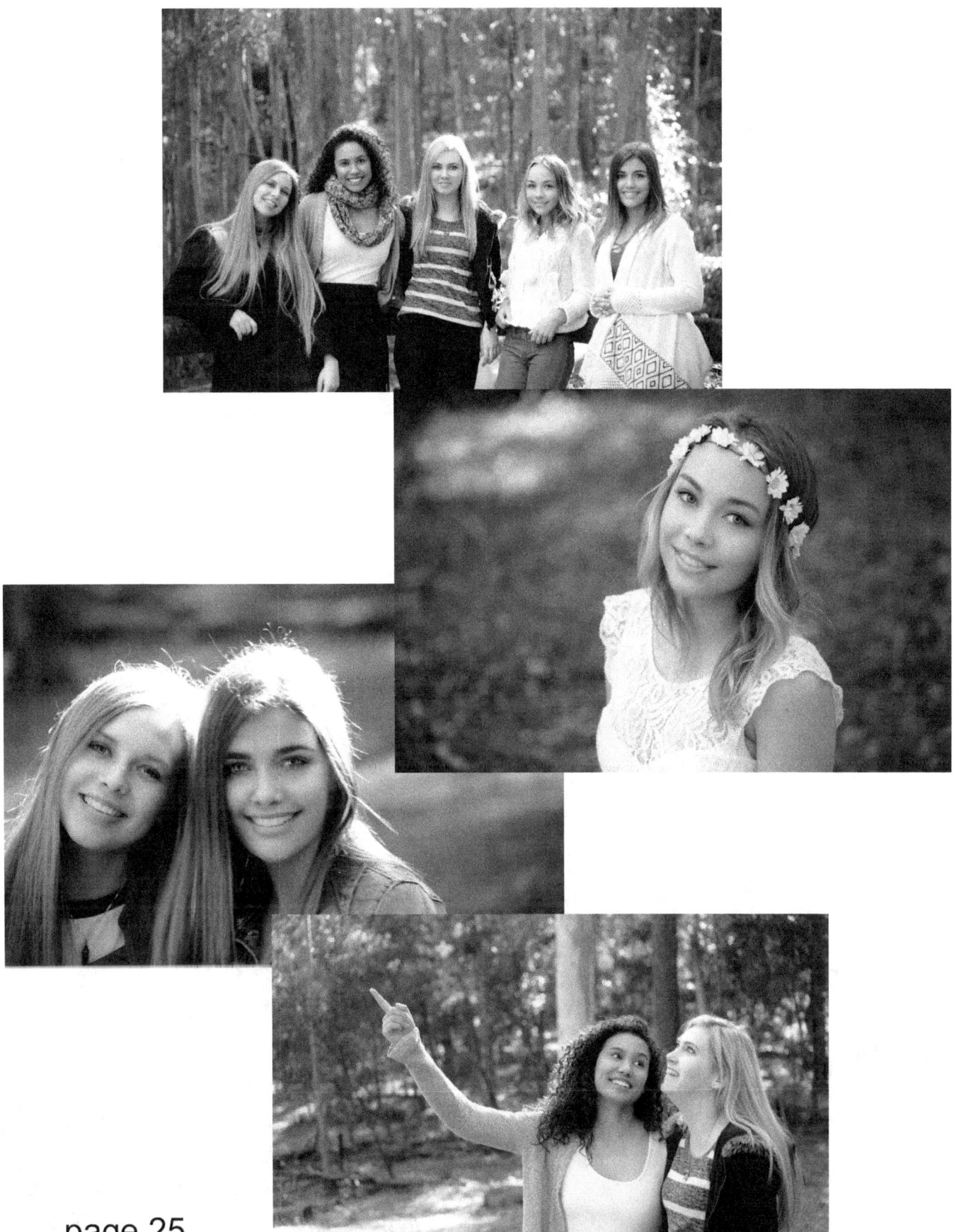

page 25

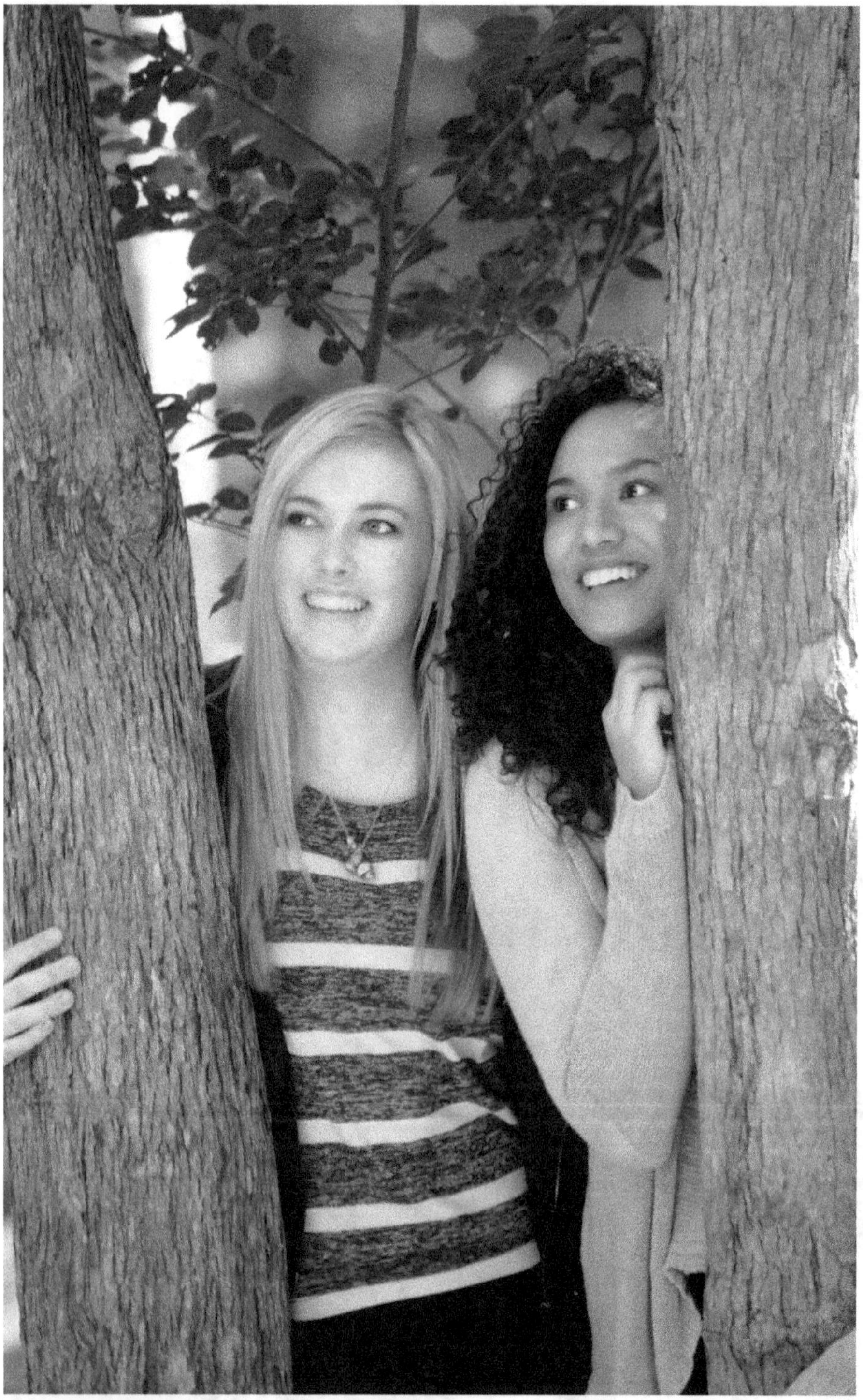

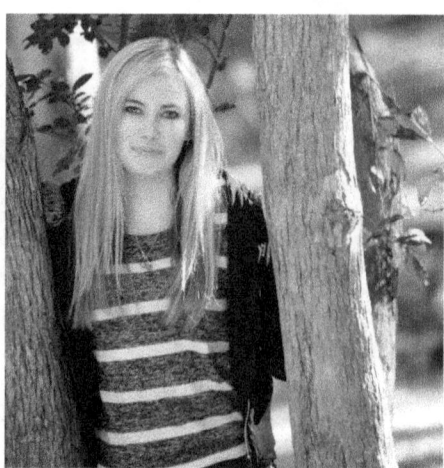
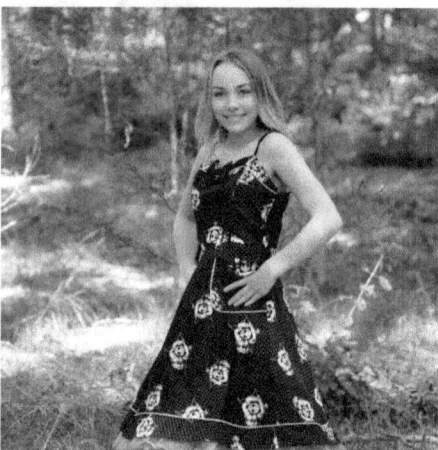
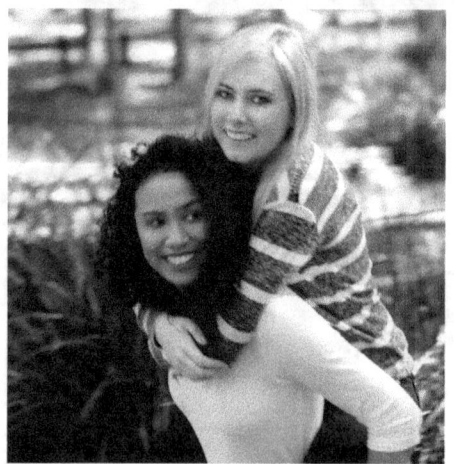
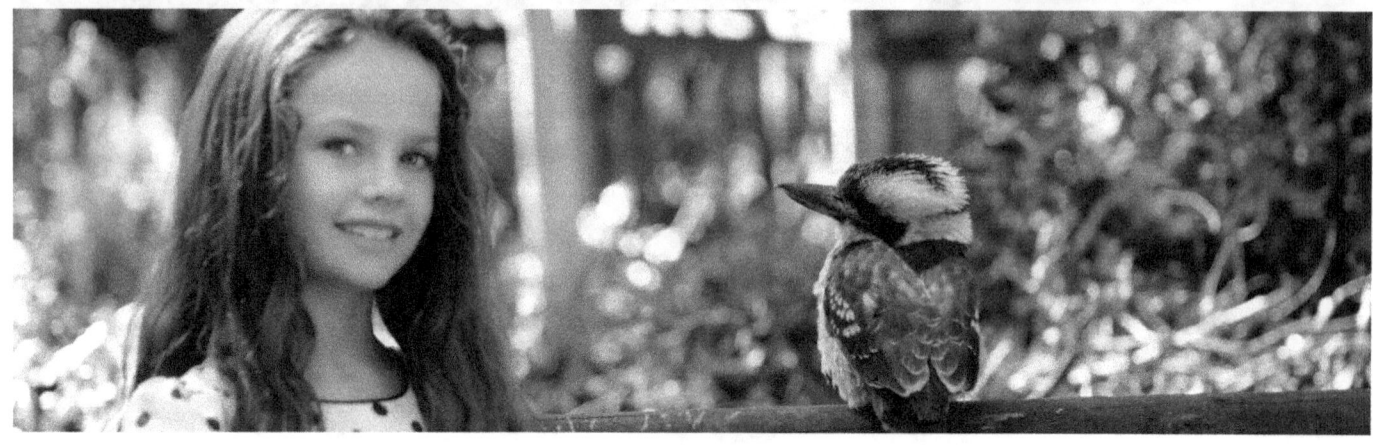

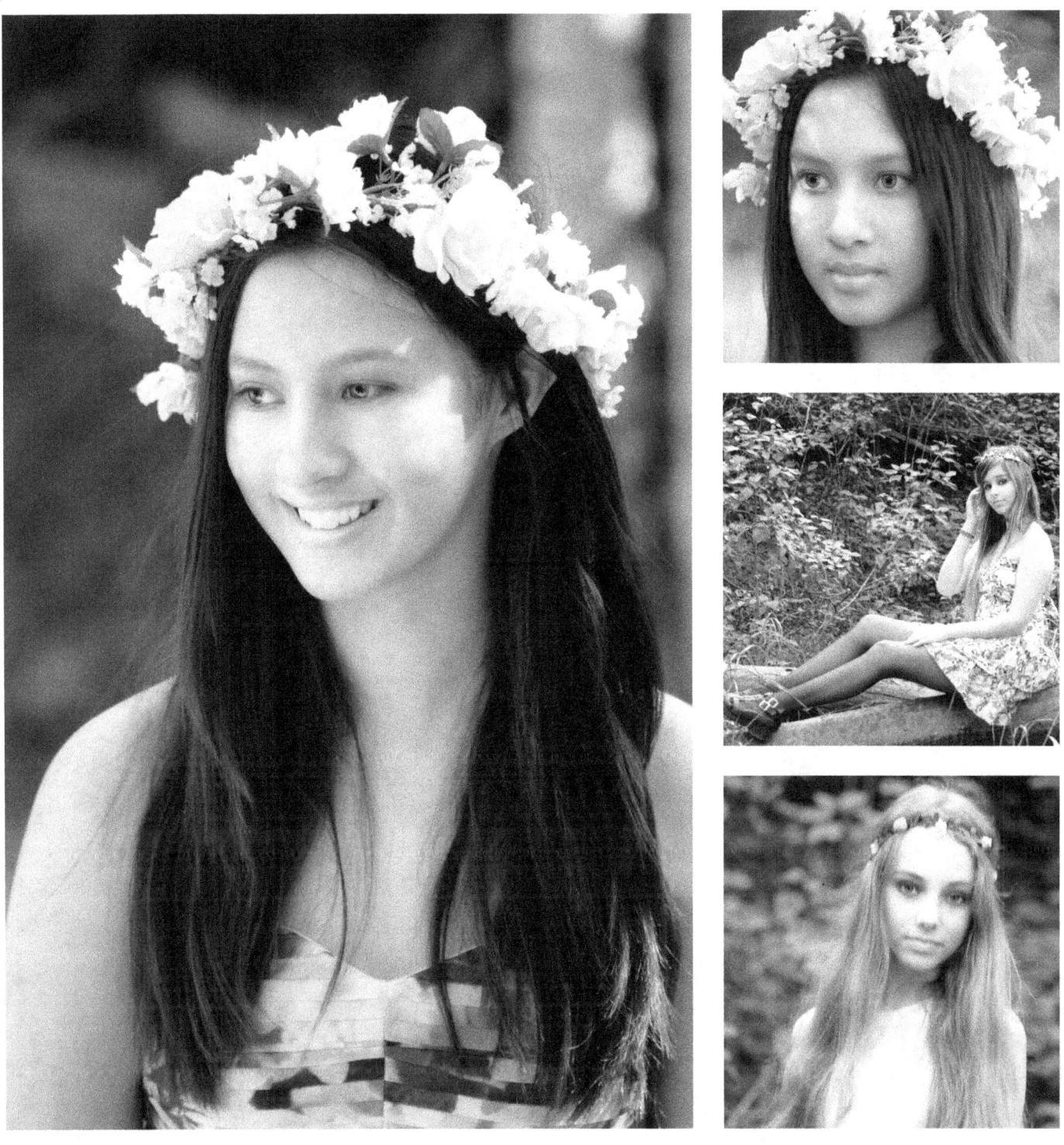

"Fairies in the Forest" shoot at
Brisbane Forest Park.

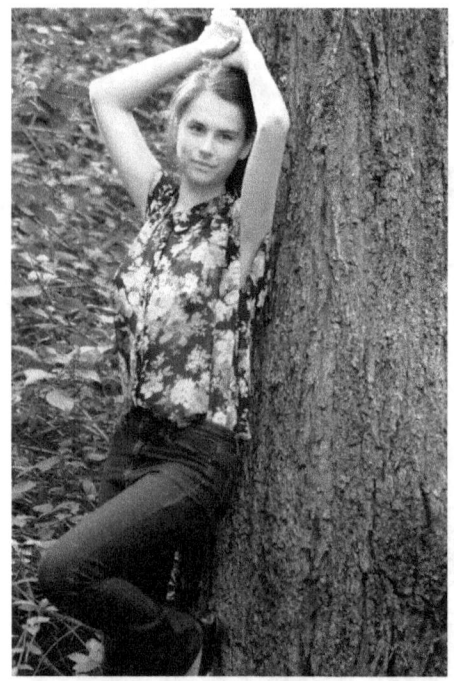
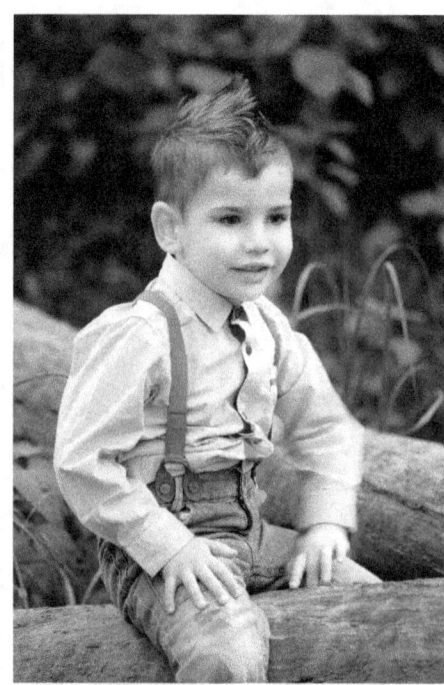
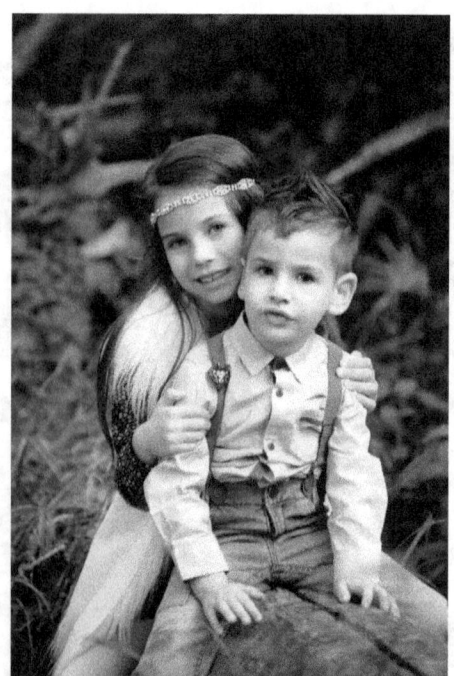
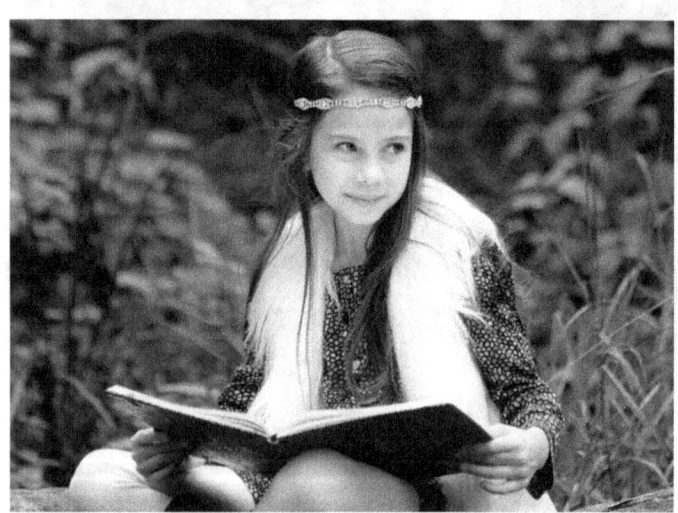
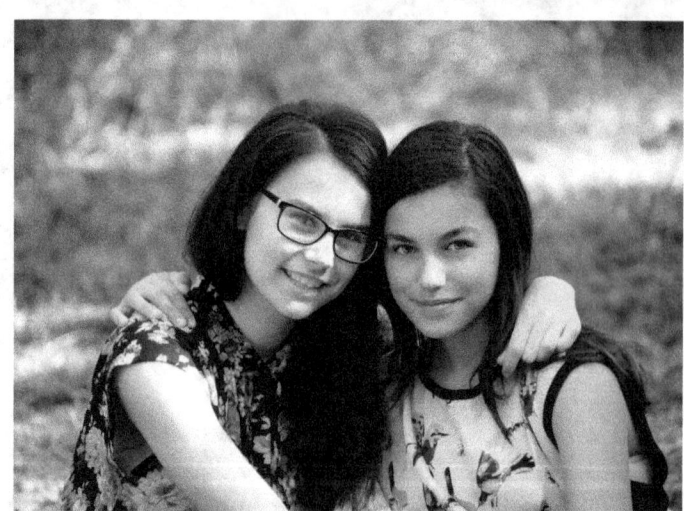
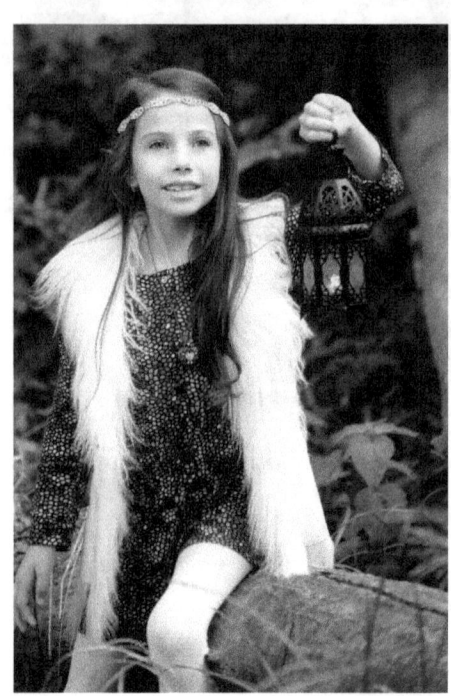
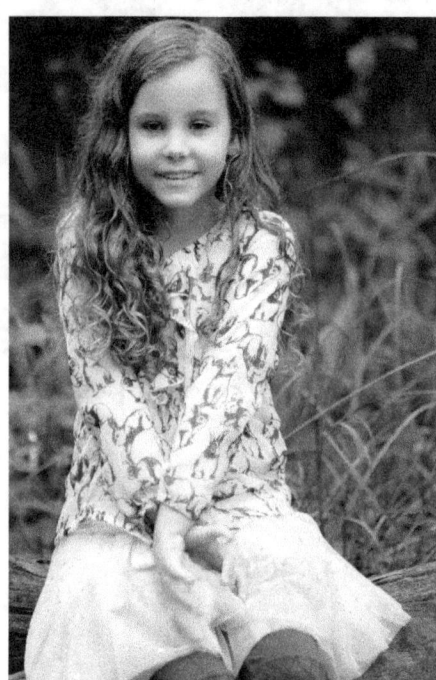
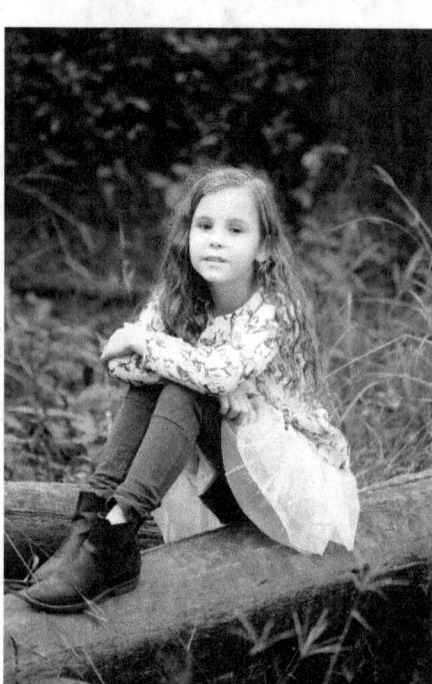

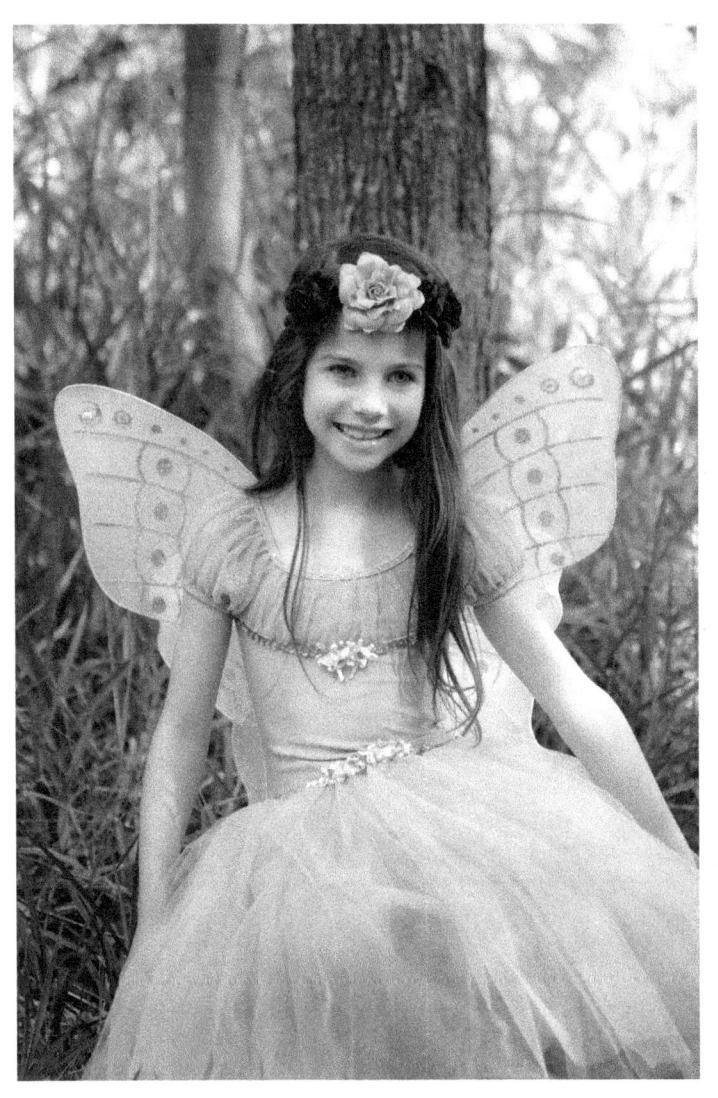

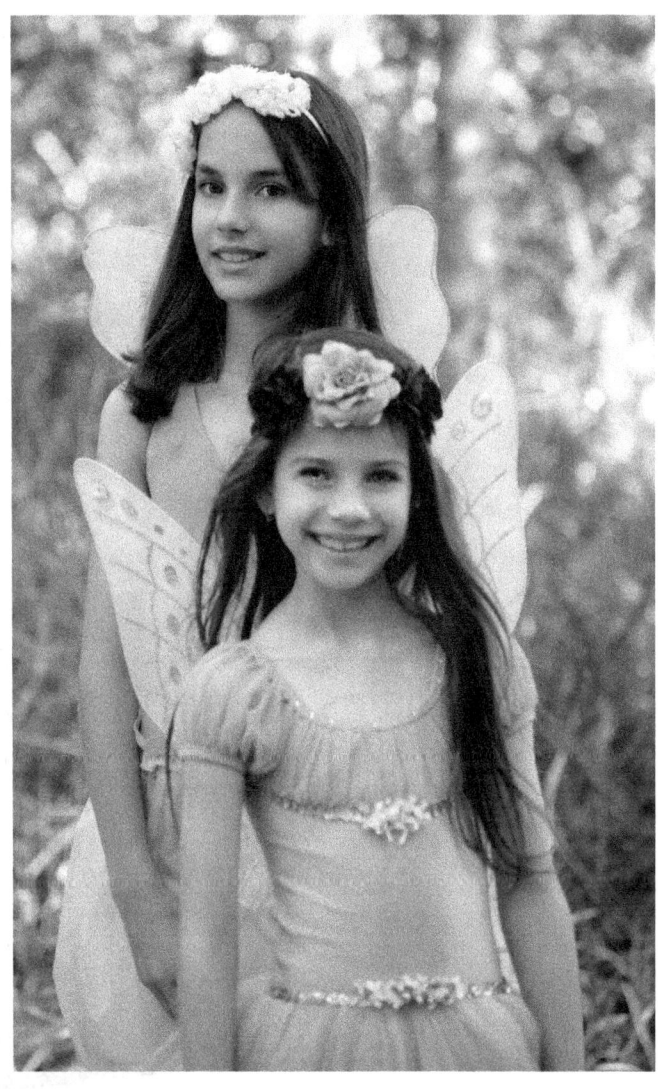

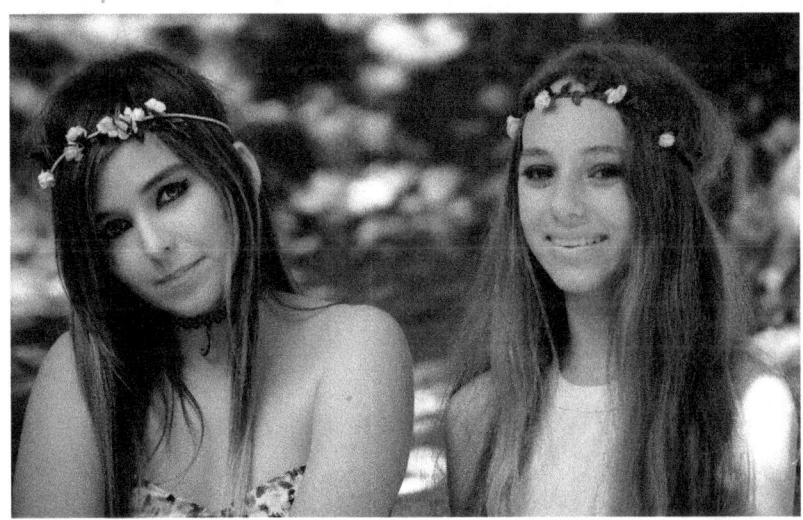

page 29

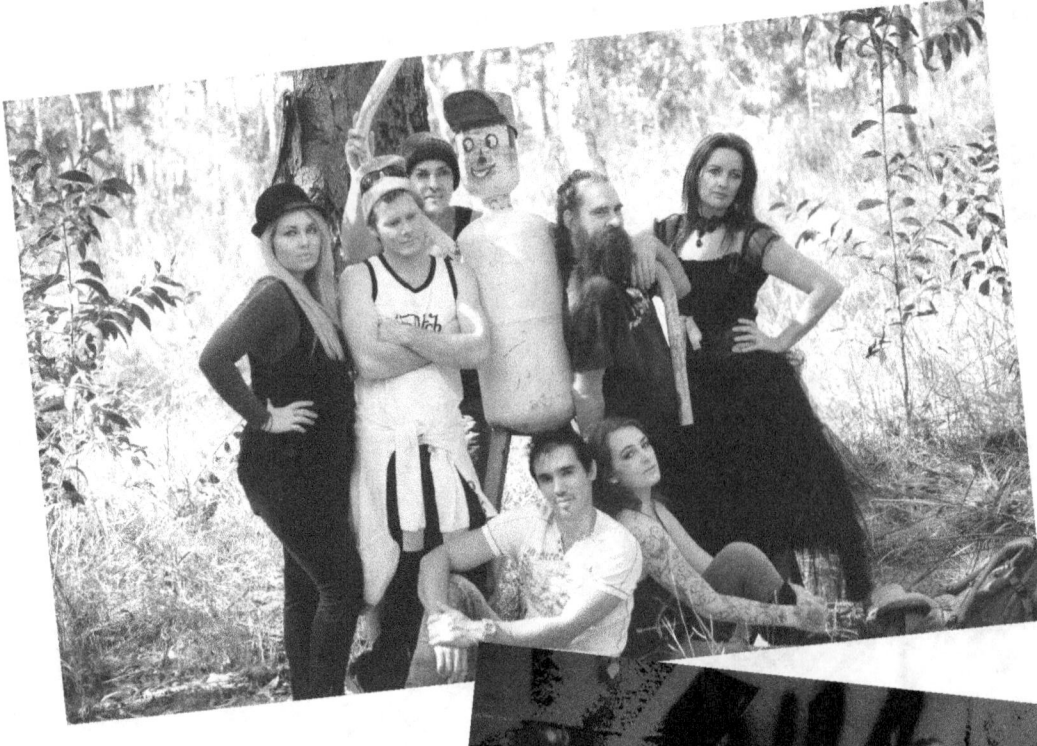

Grunge Shoot
Browns Plains

page 30

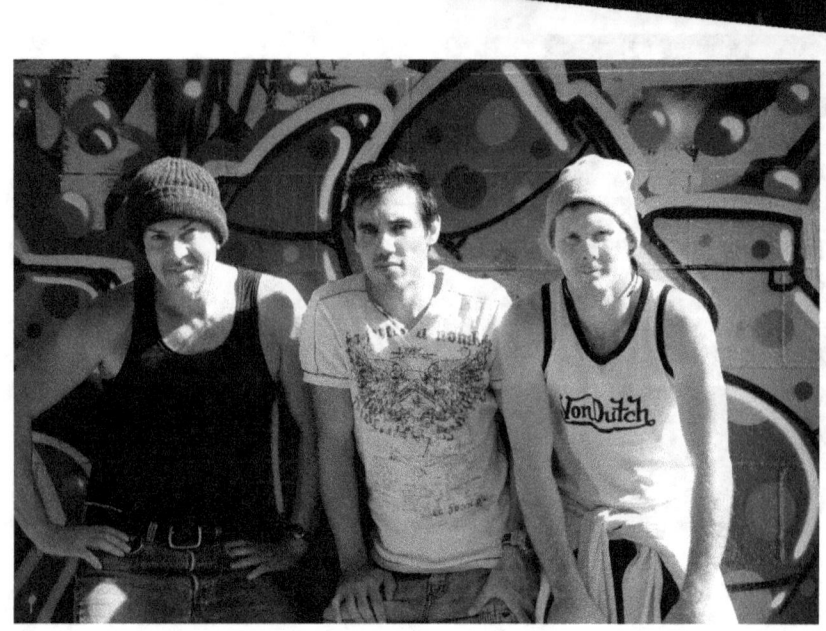

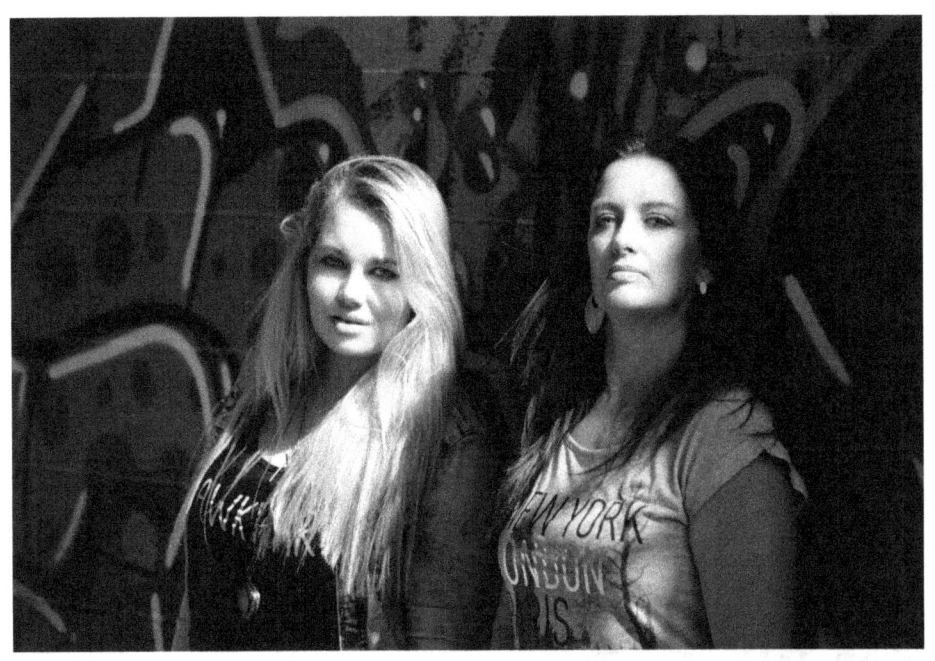

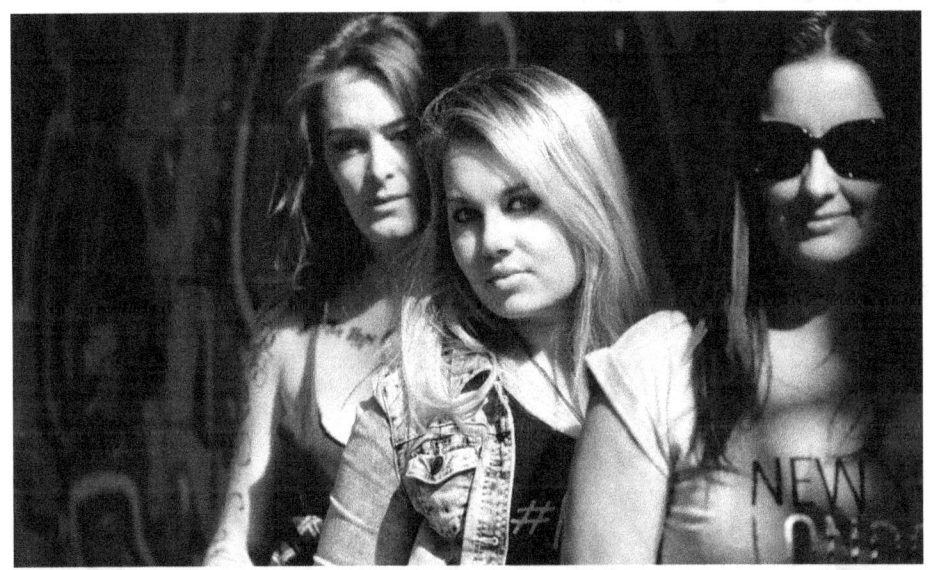

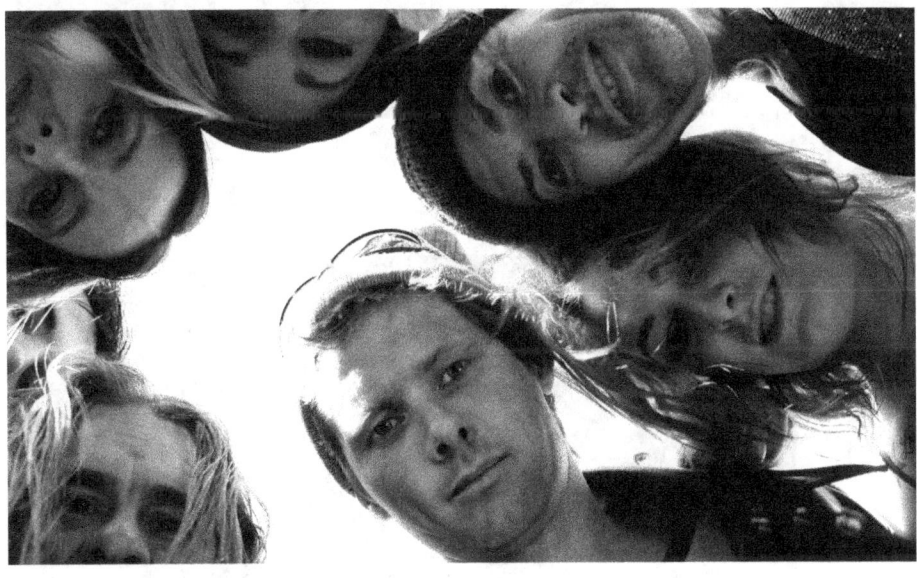

page 31

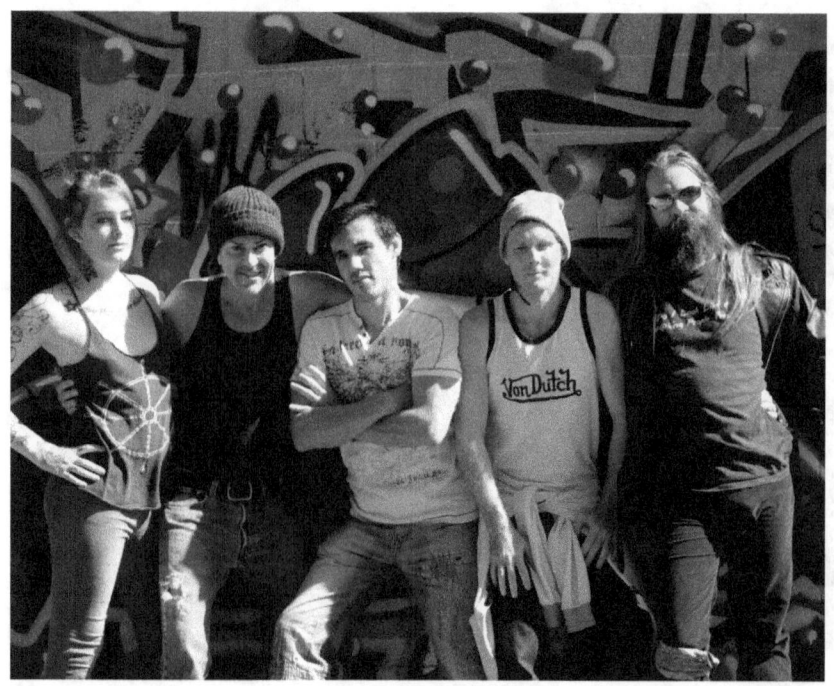

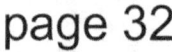

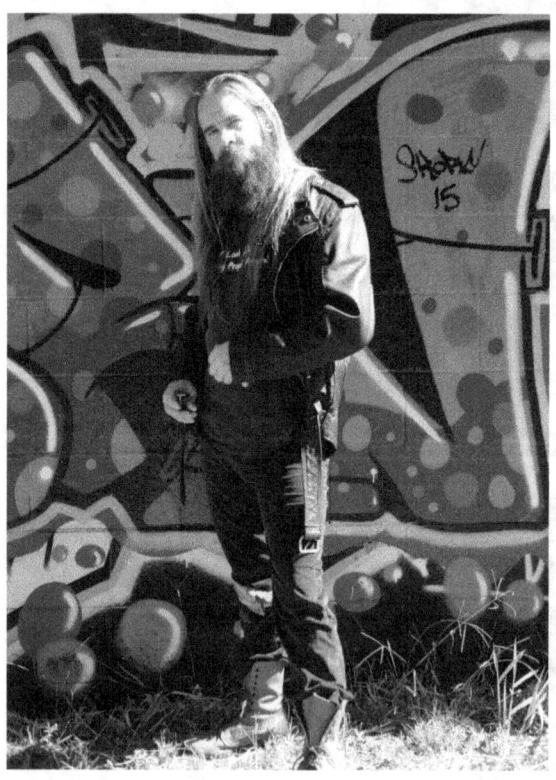

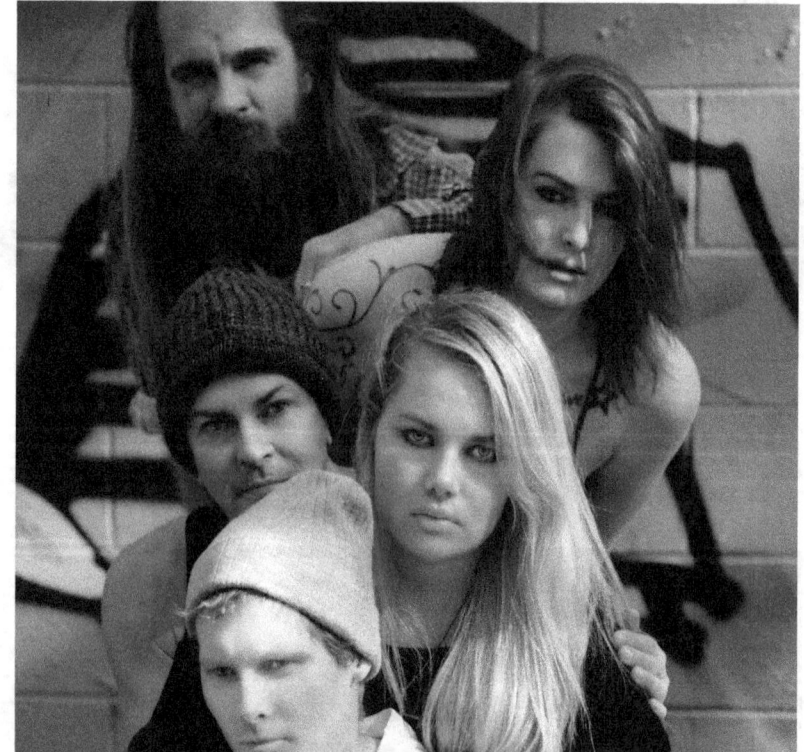

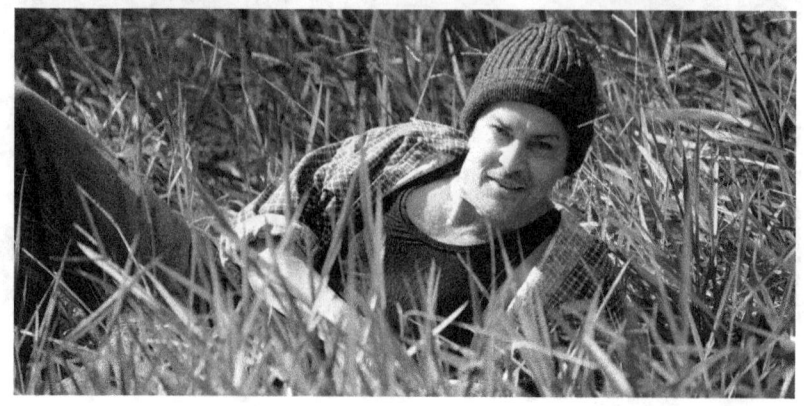

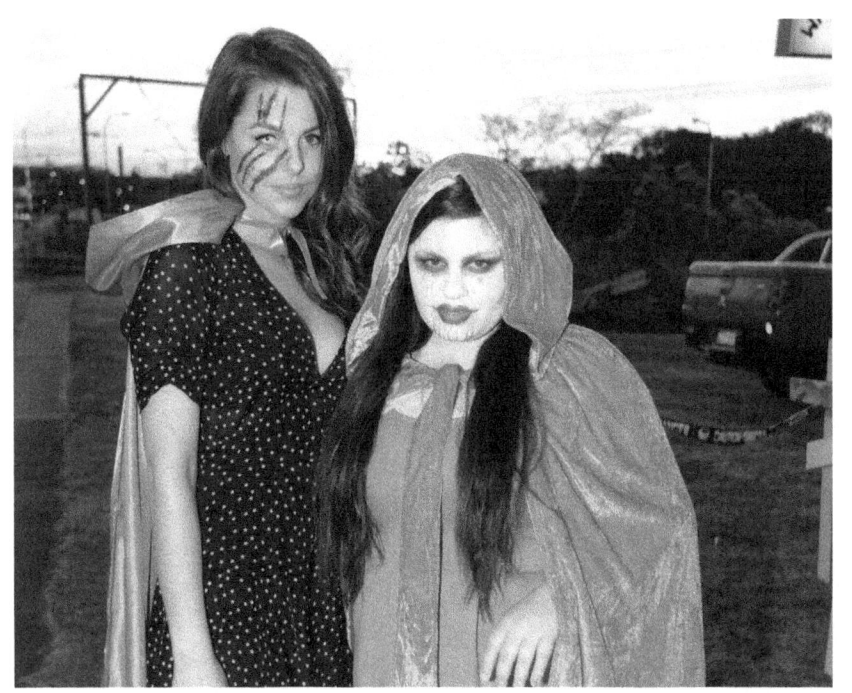

Halloween Shoot

page 33

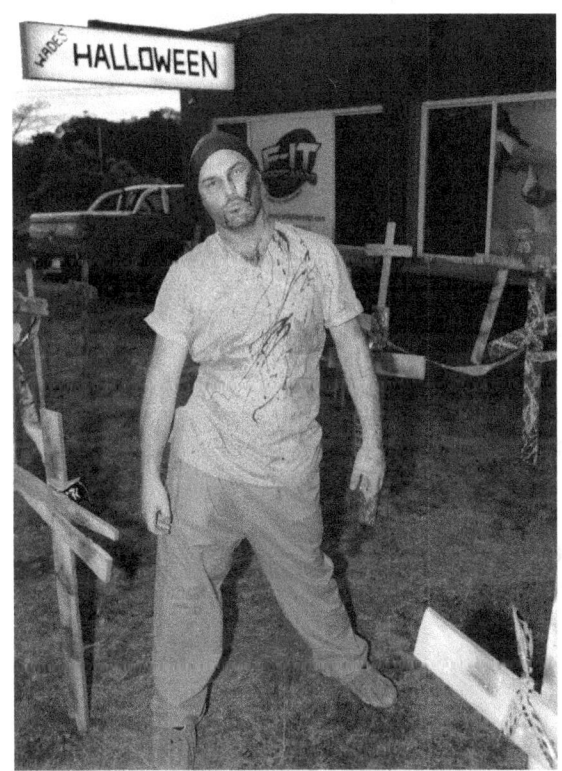

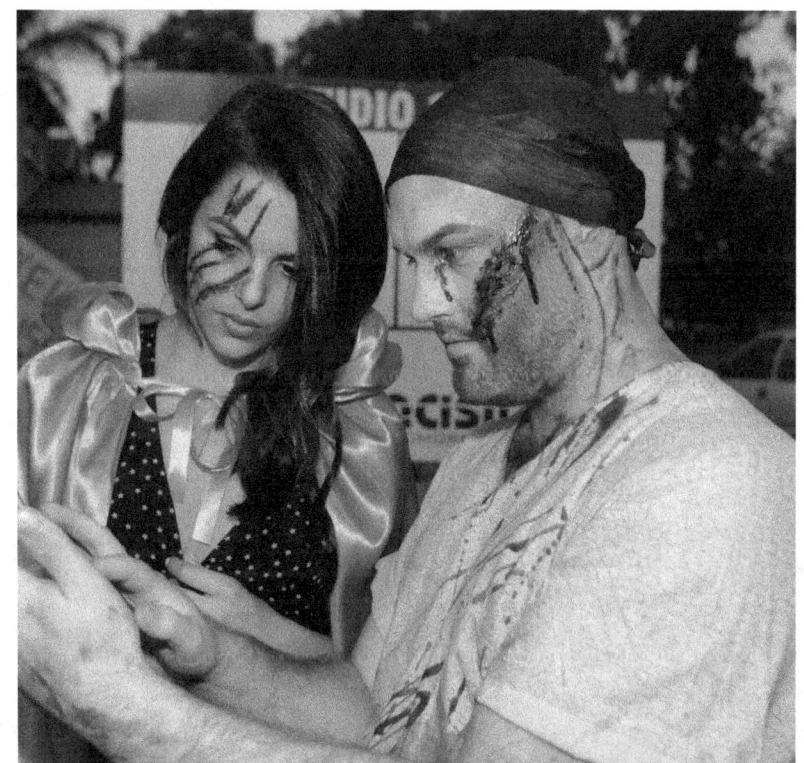

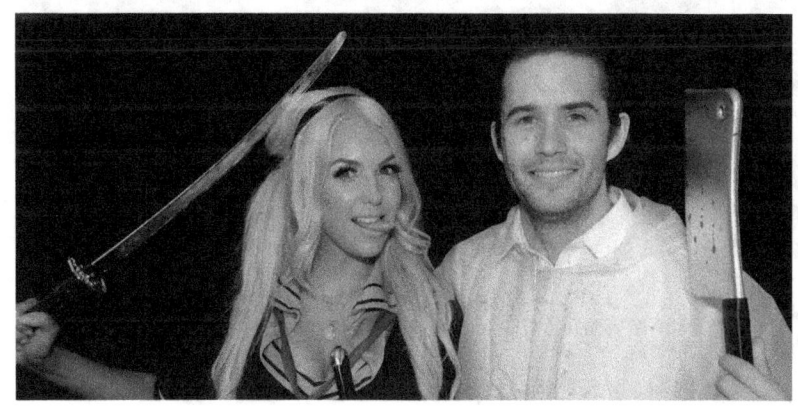

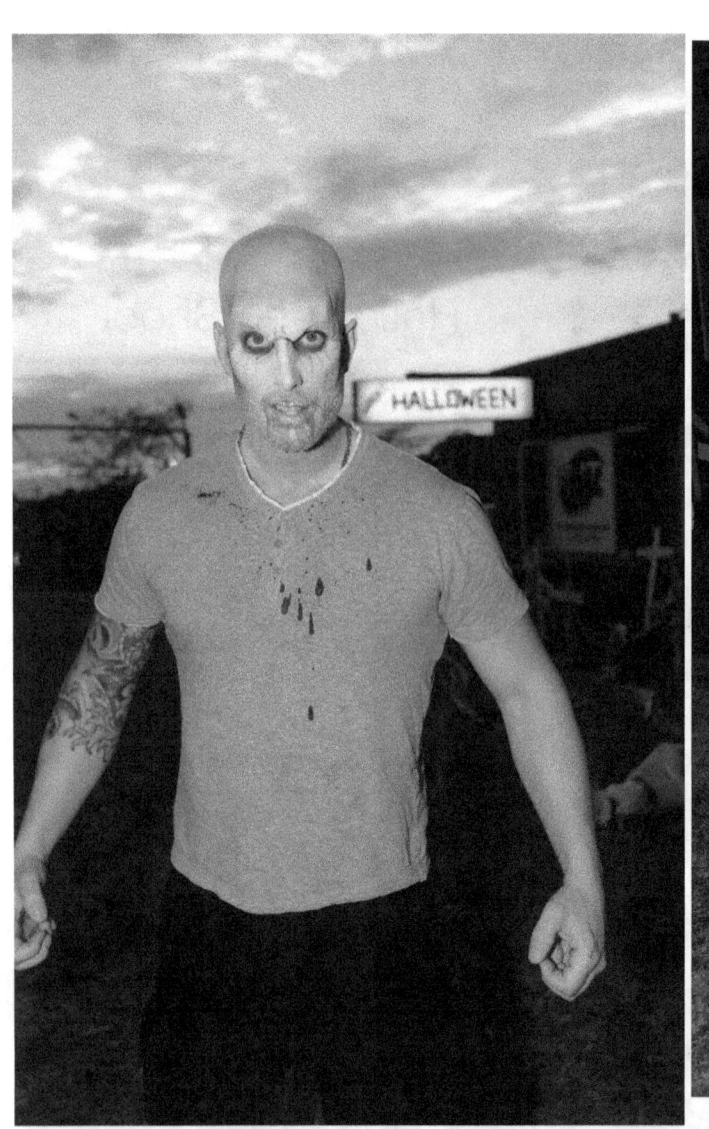
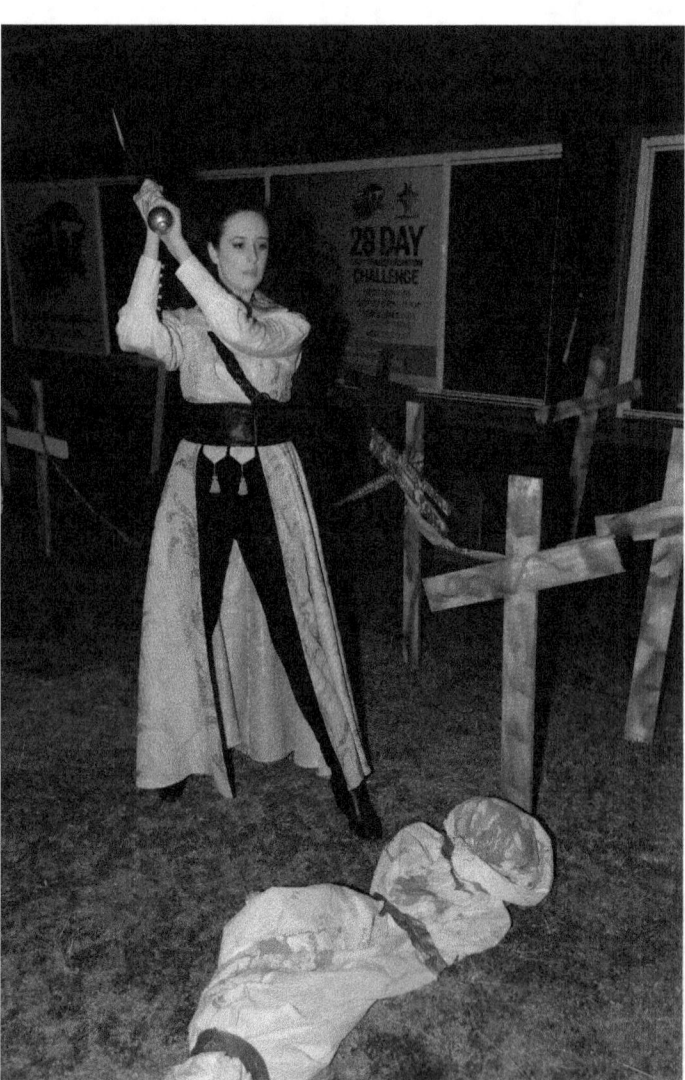
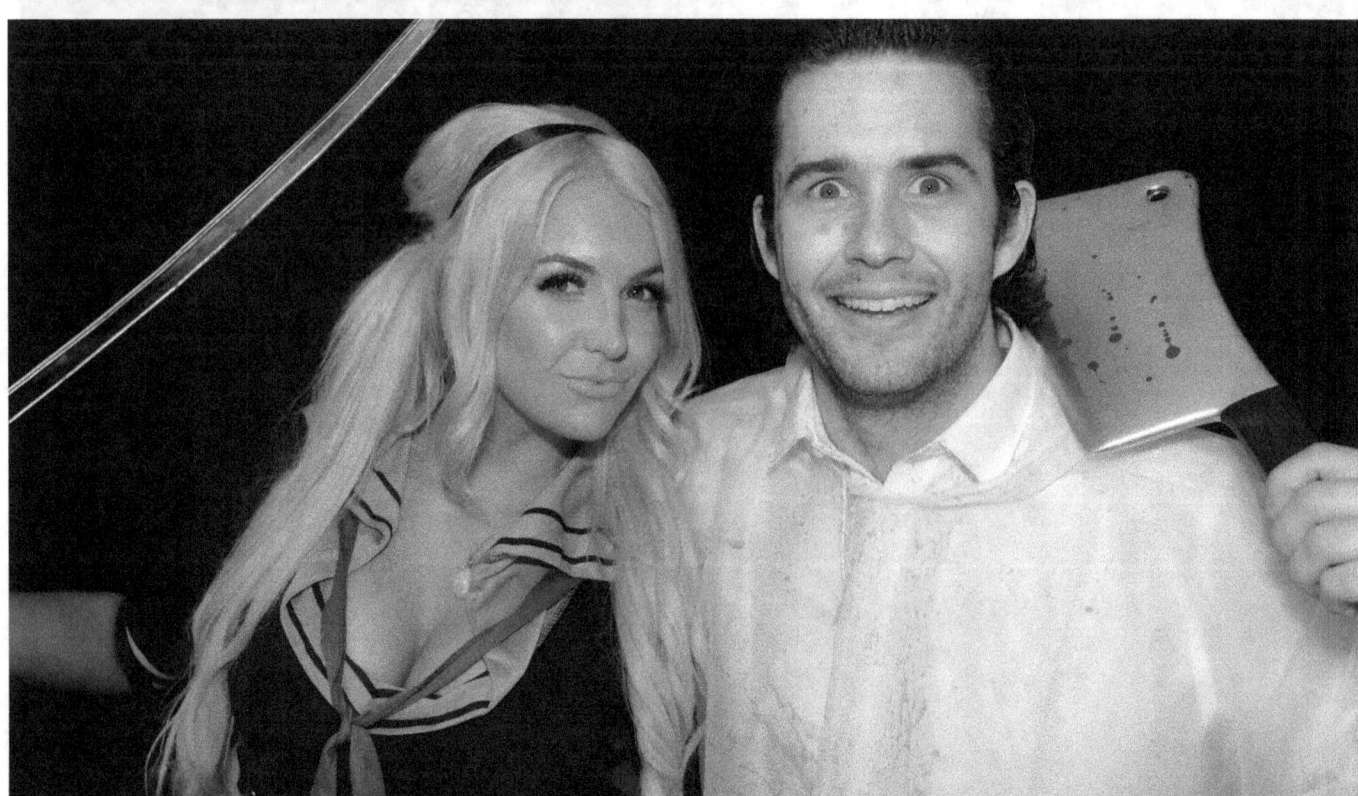

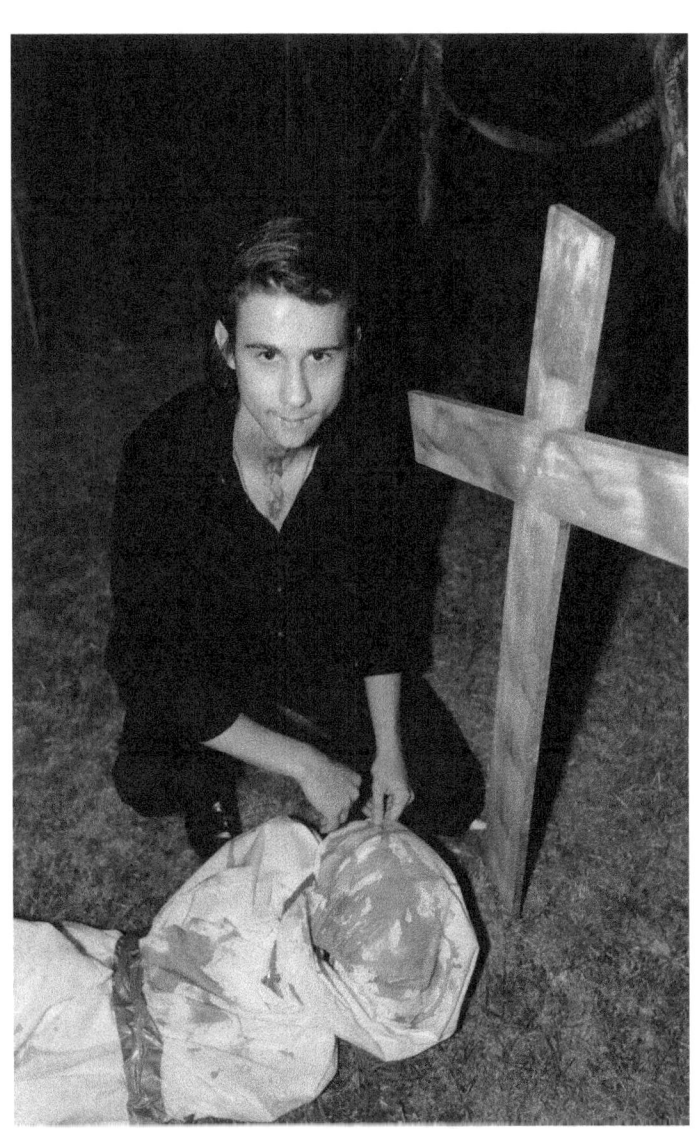
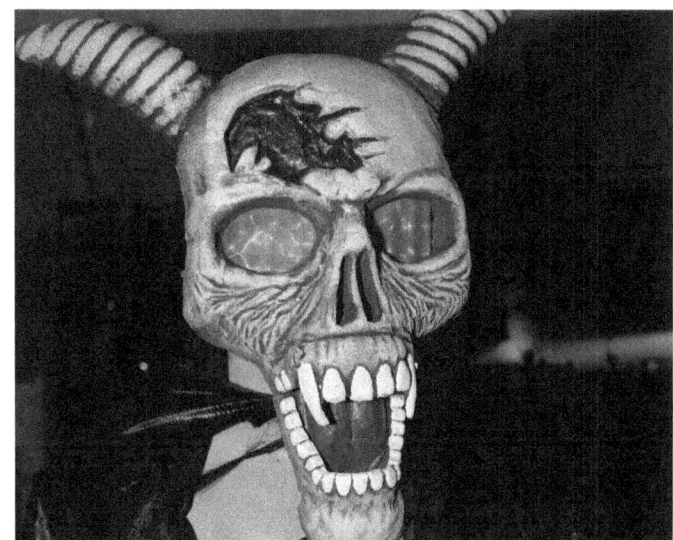
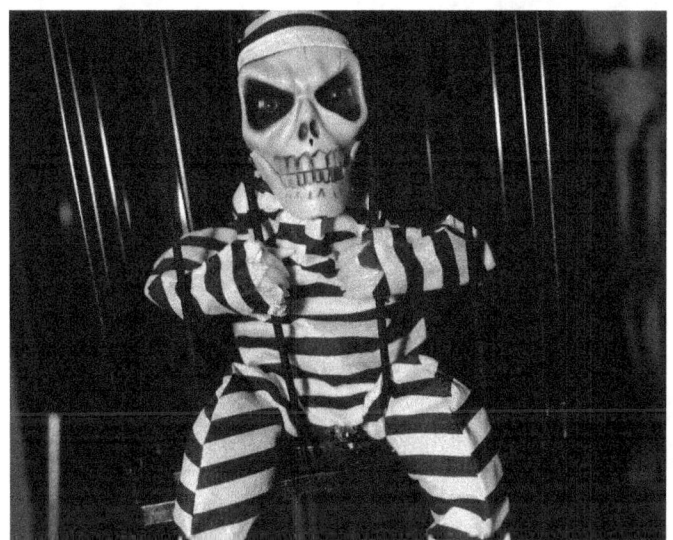
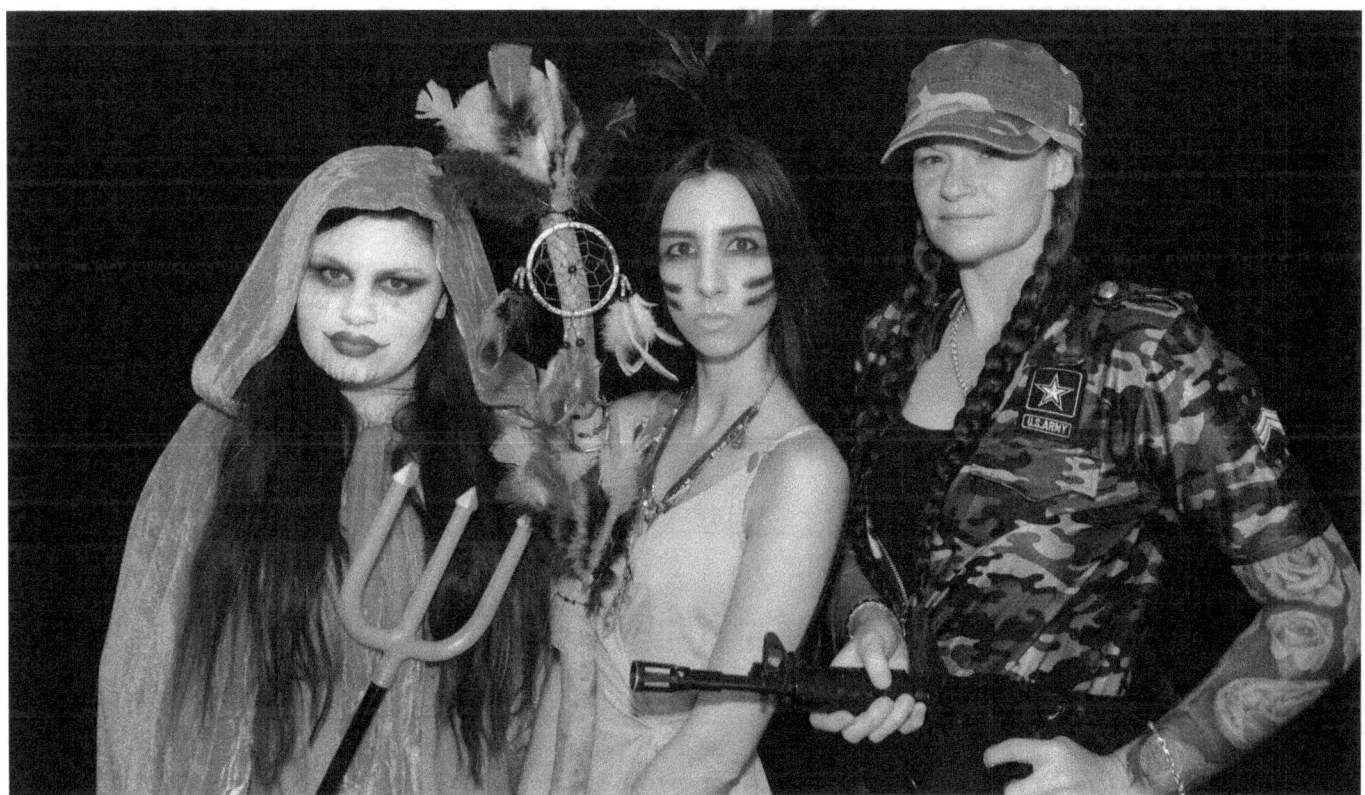

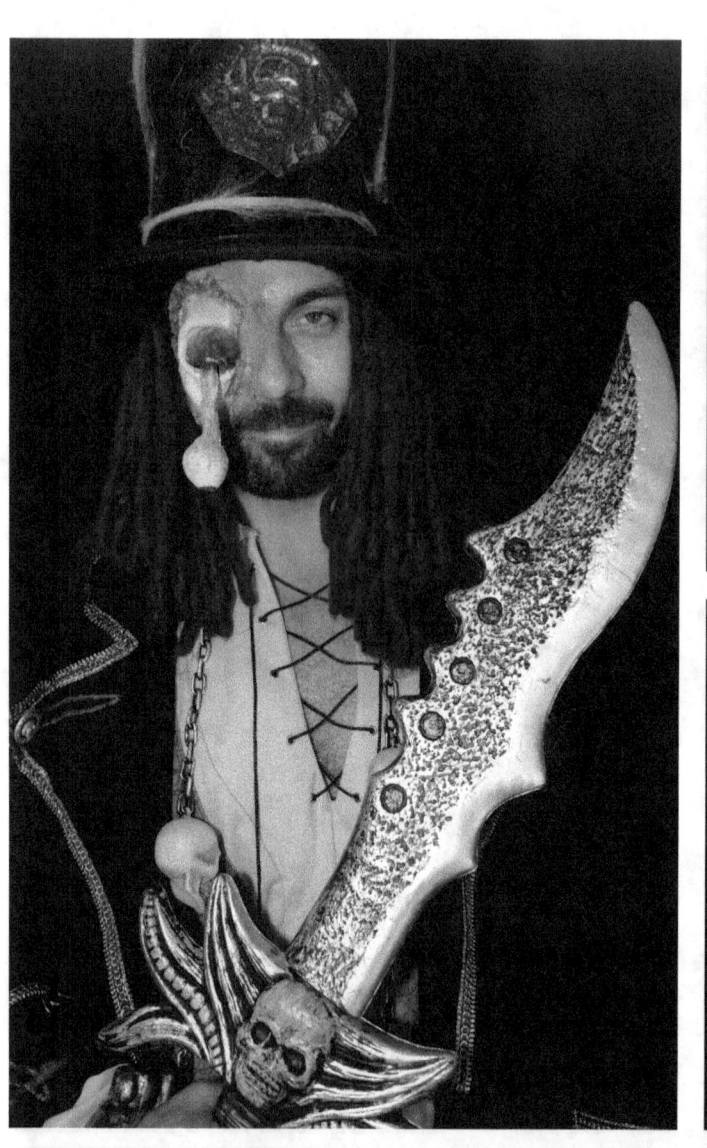
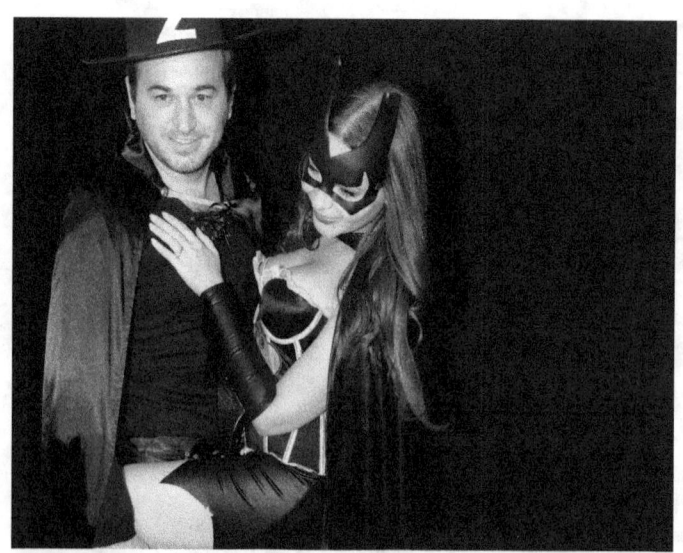
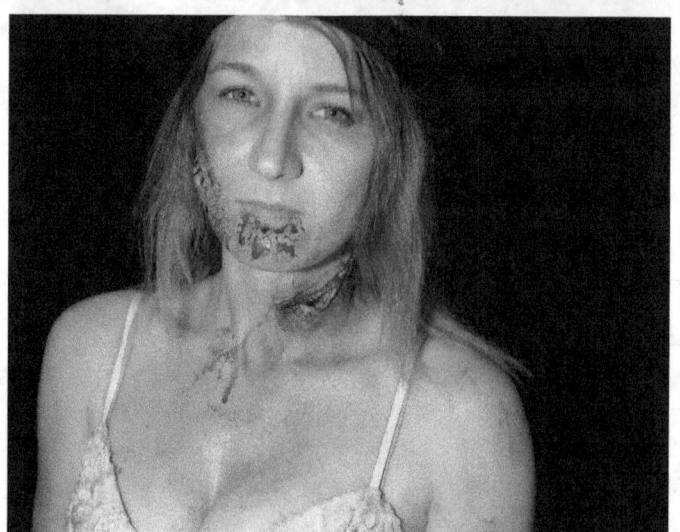
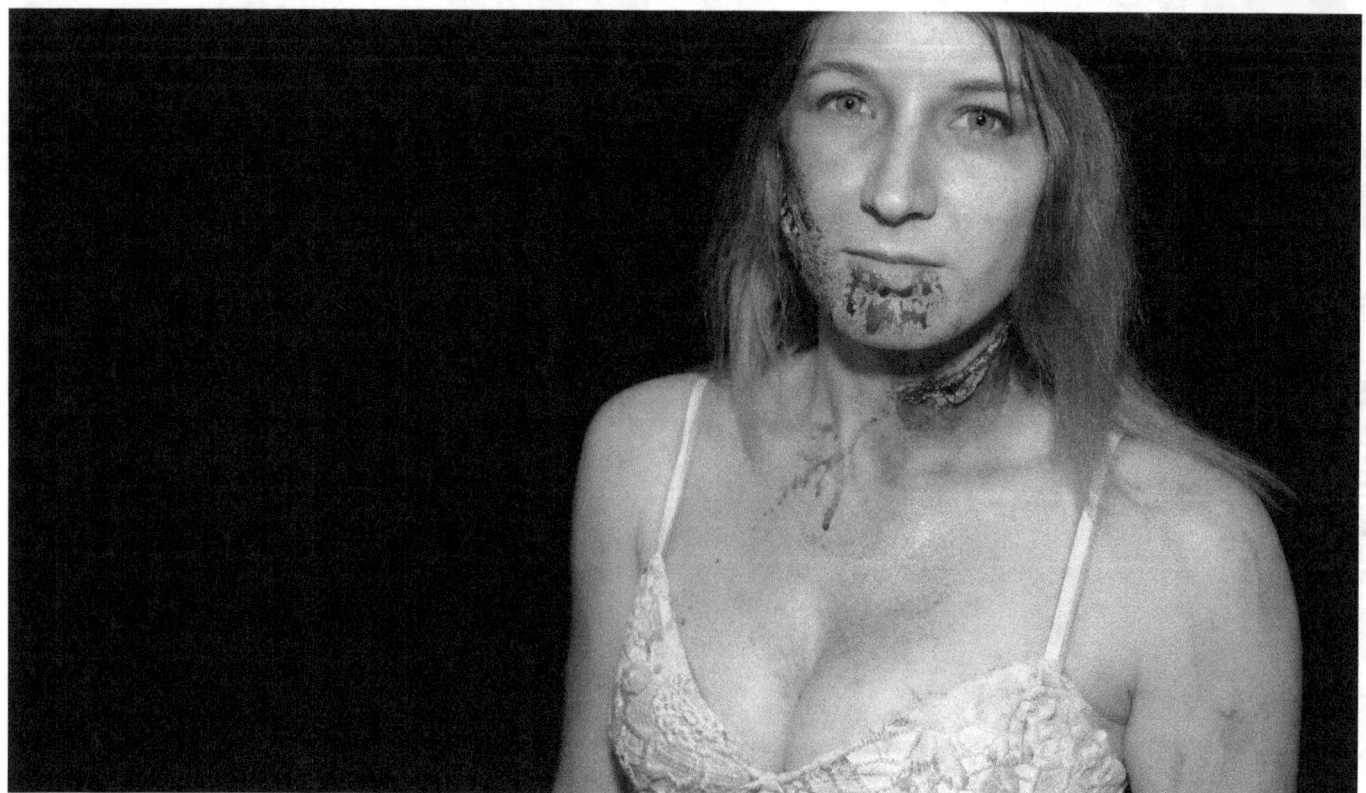

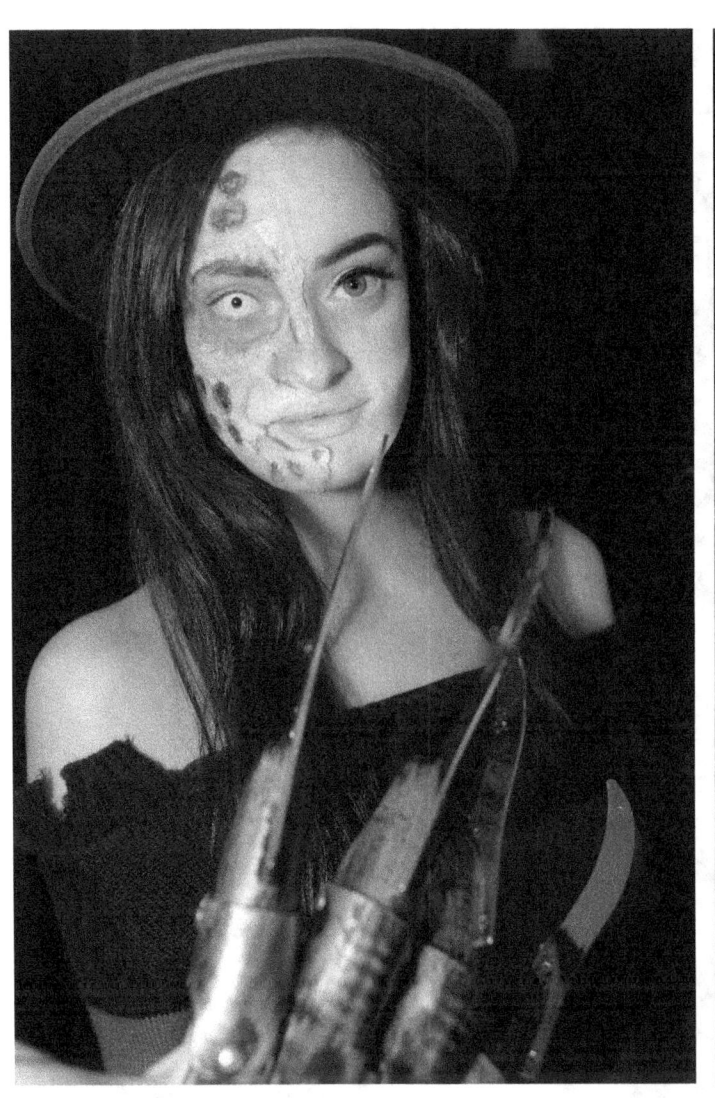

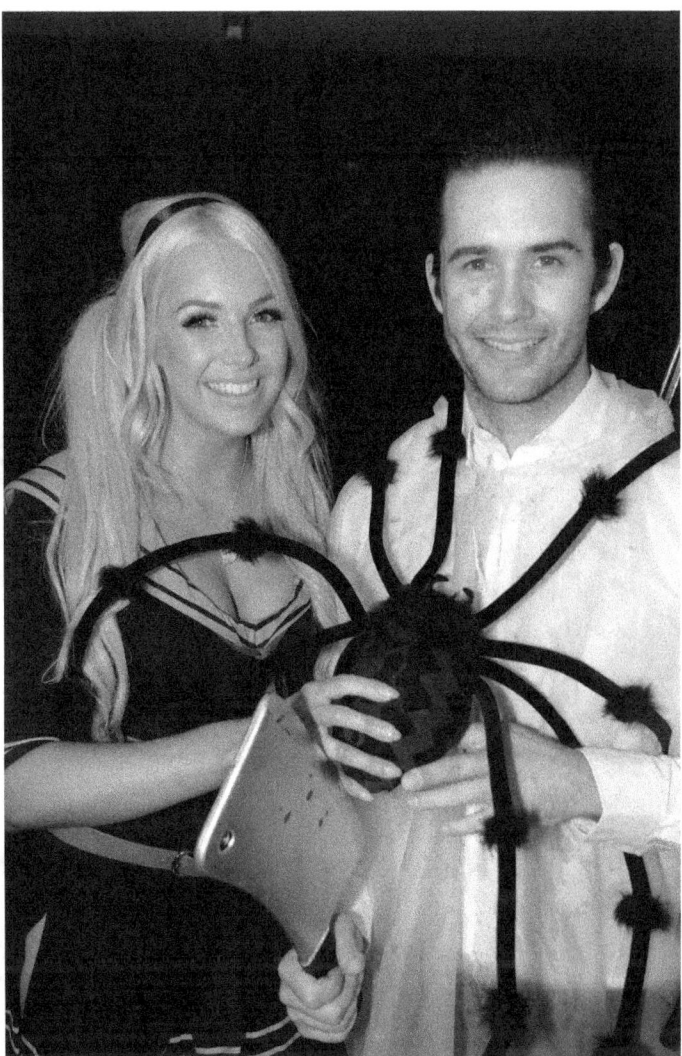

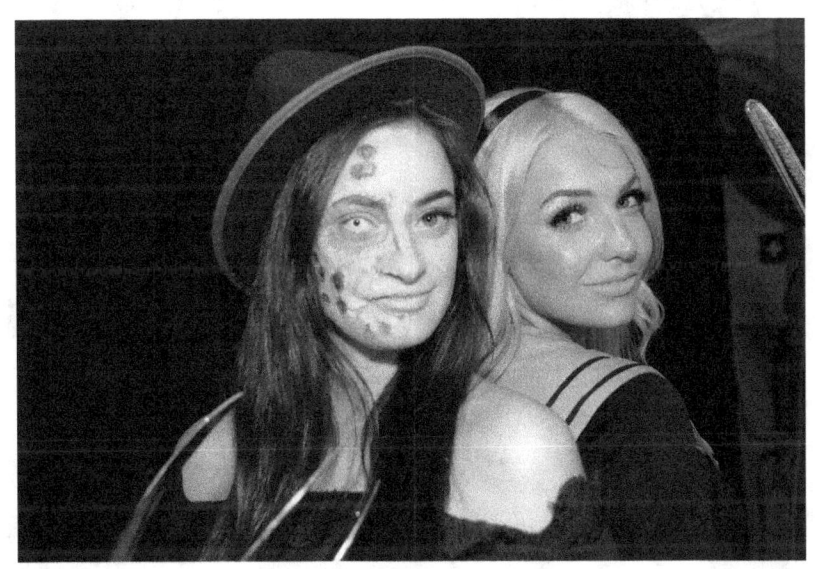

page 37

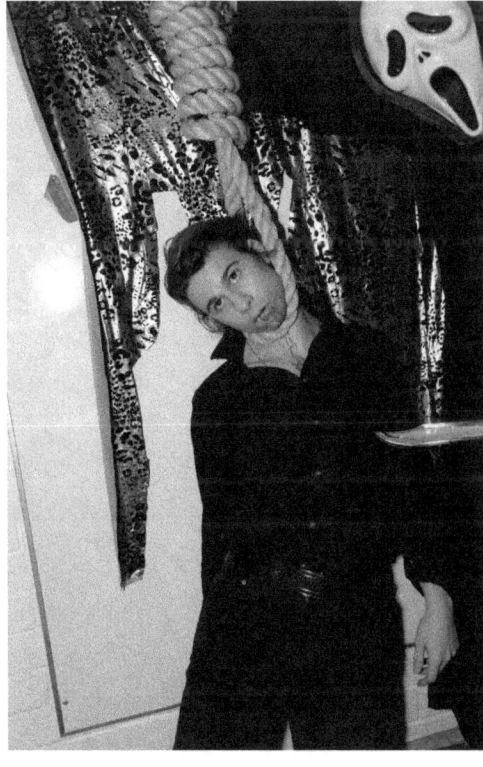

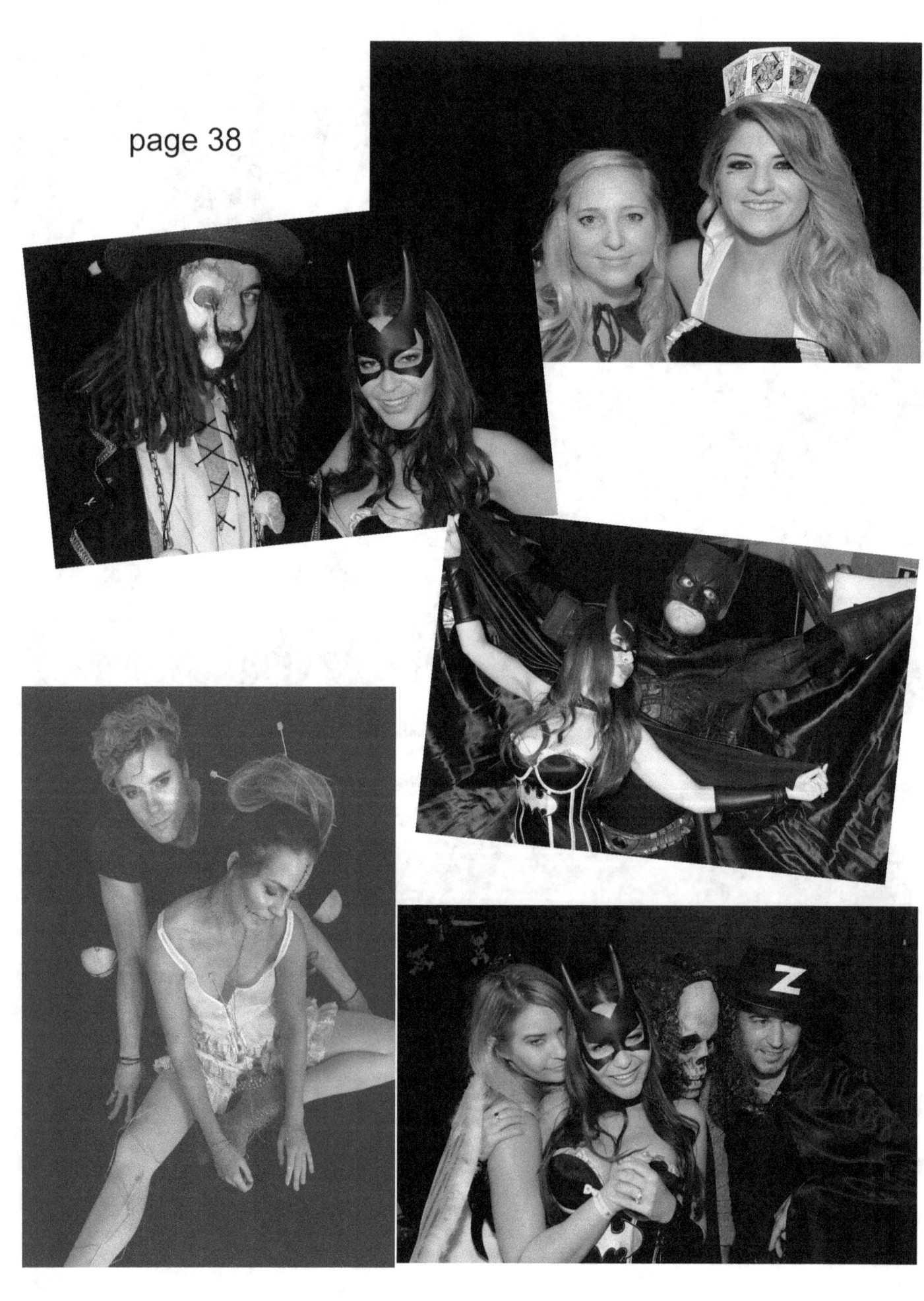

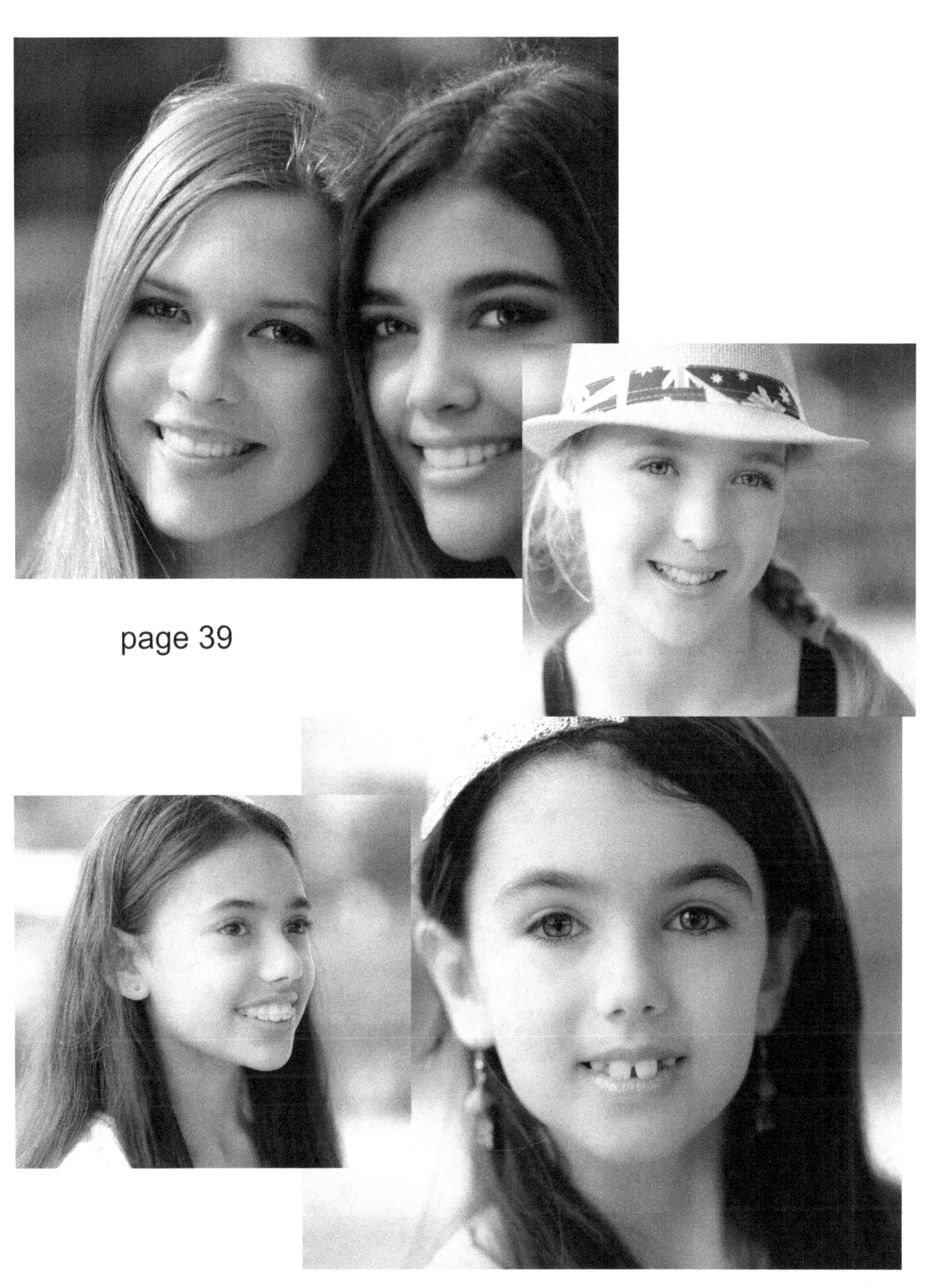

page 39

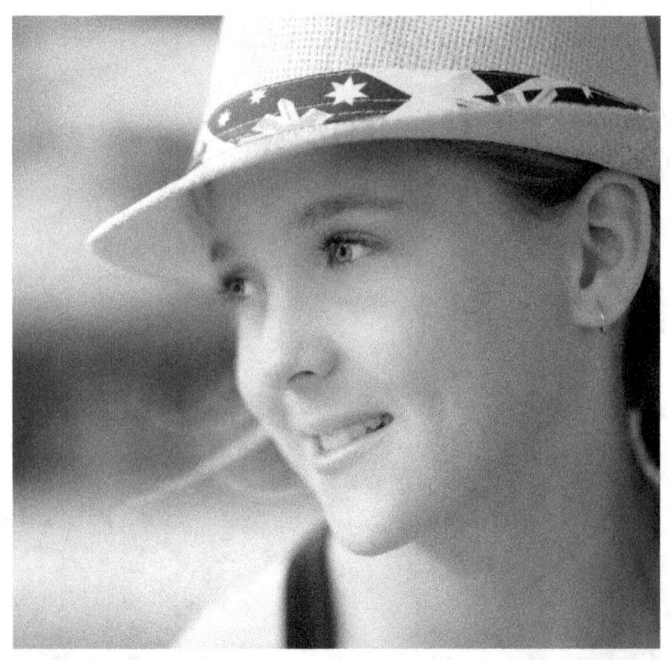

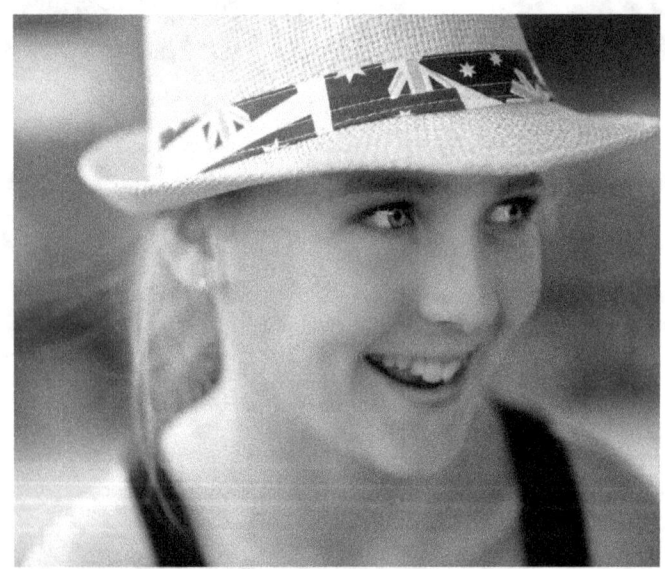

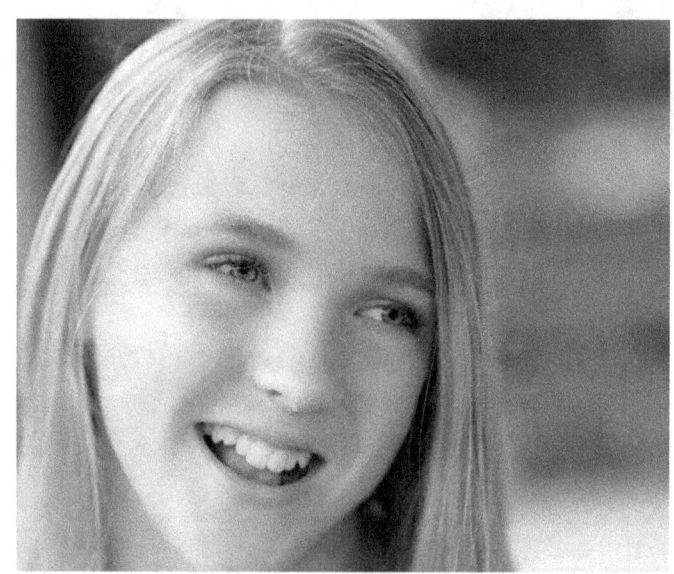

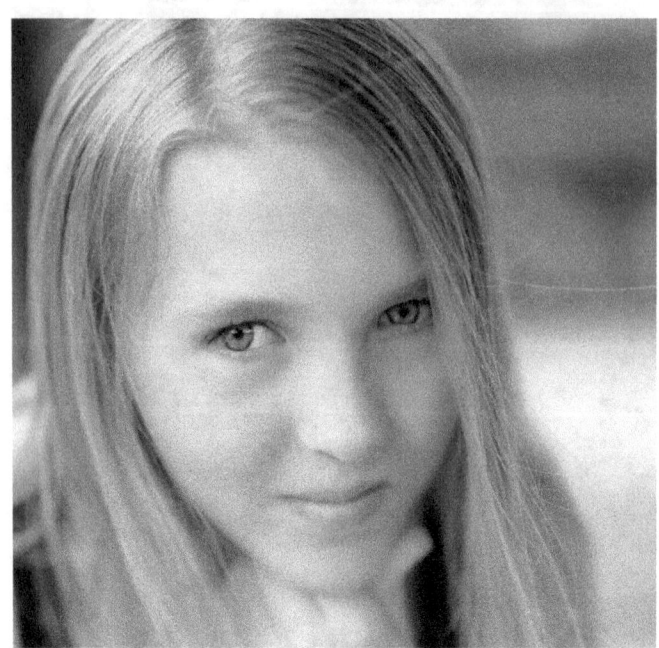

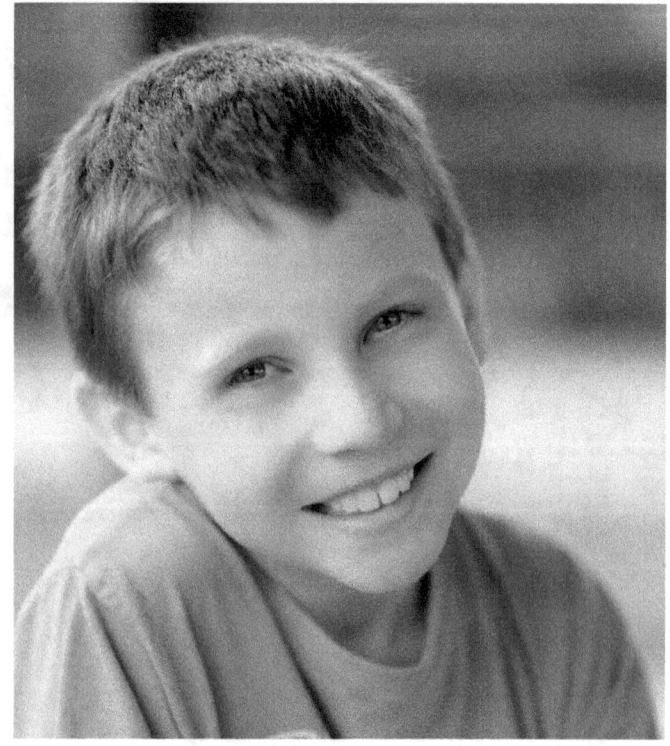

Head Shots

page 40

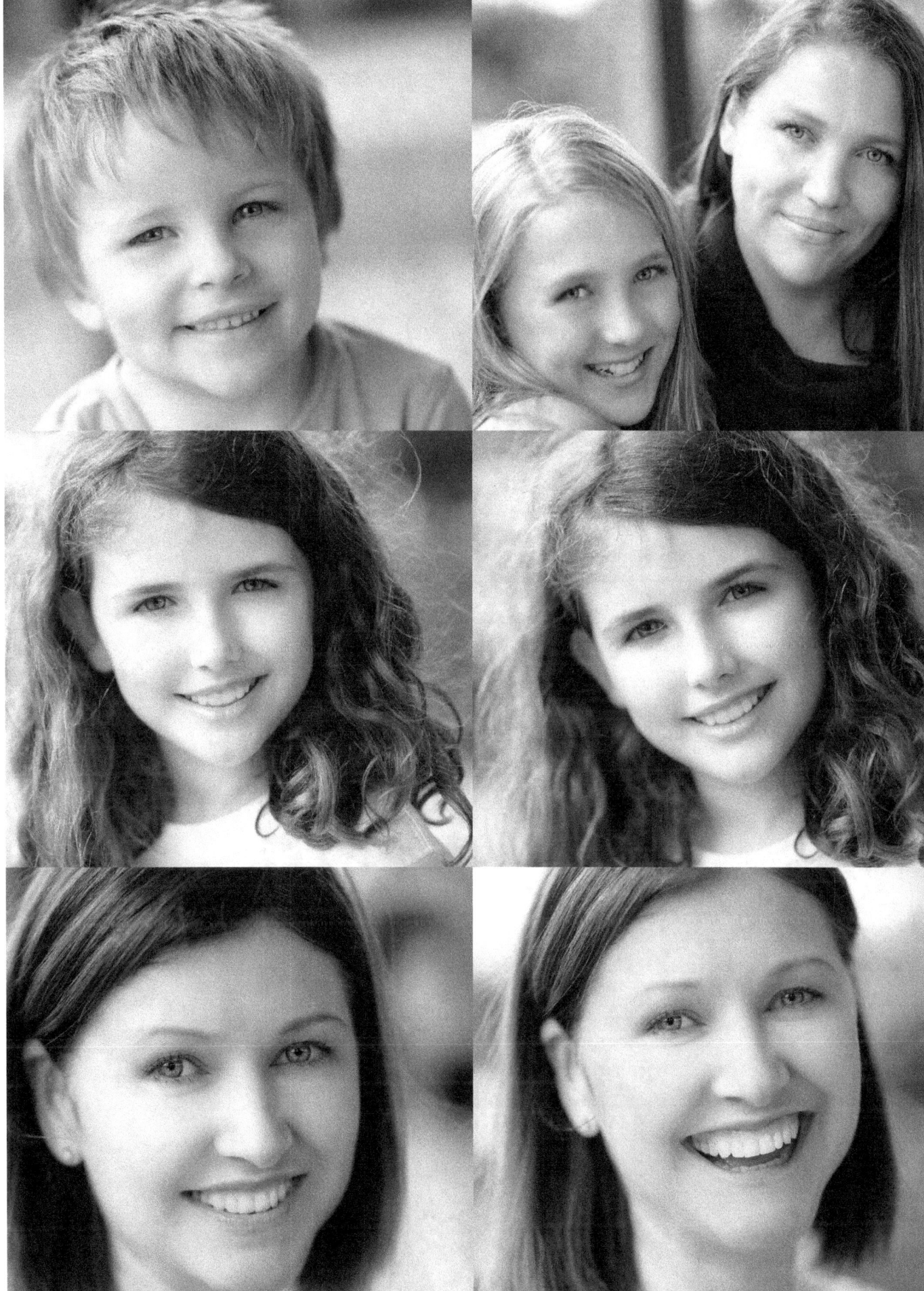

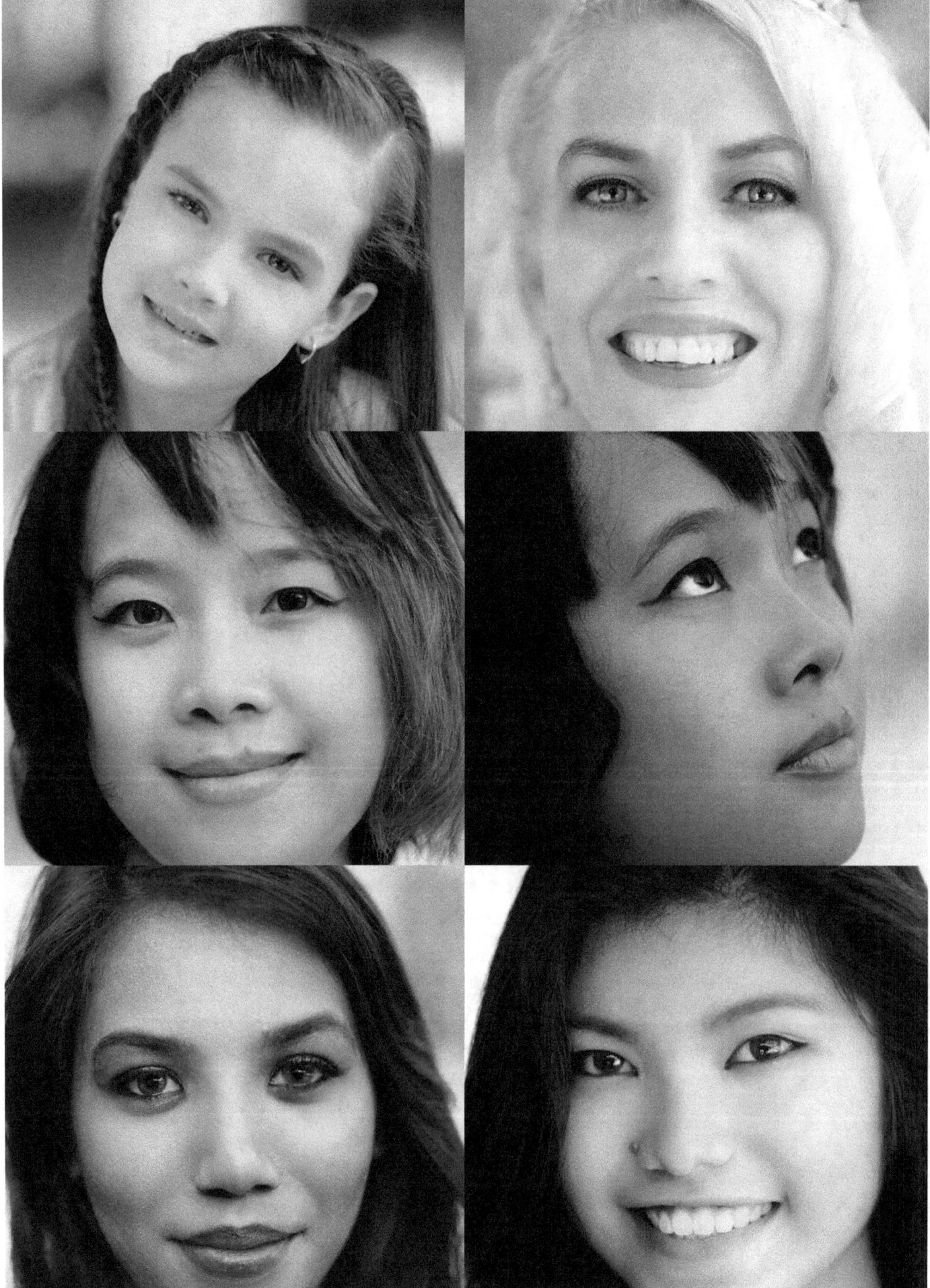

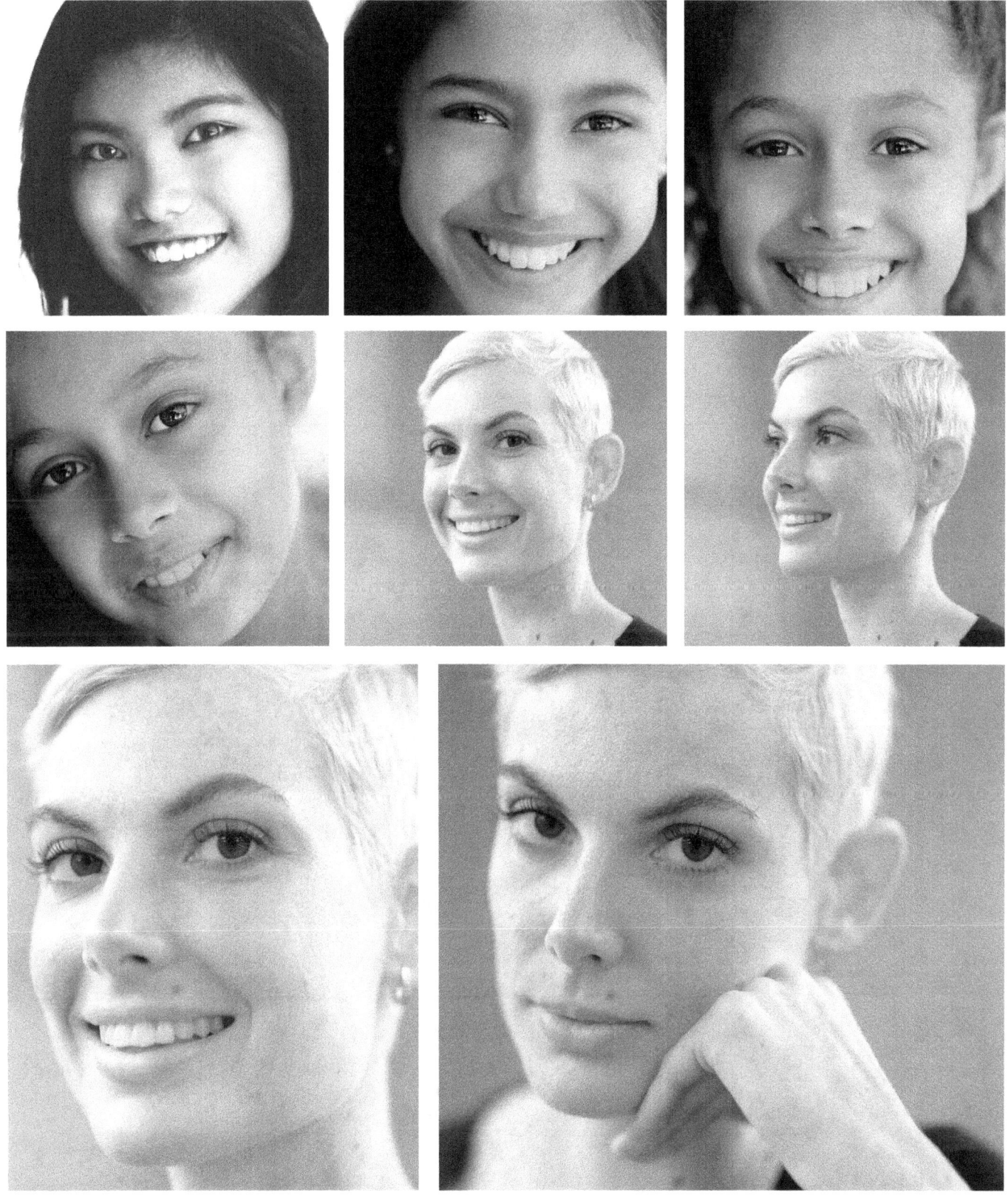

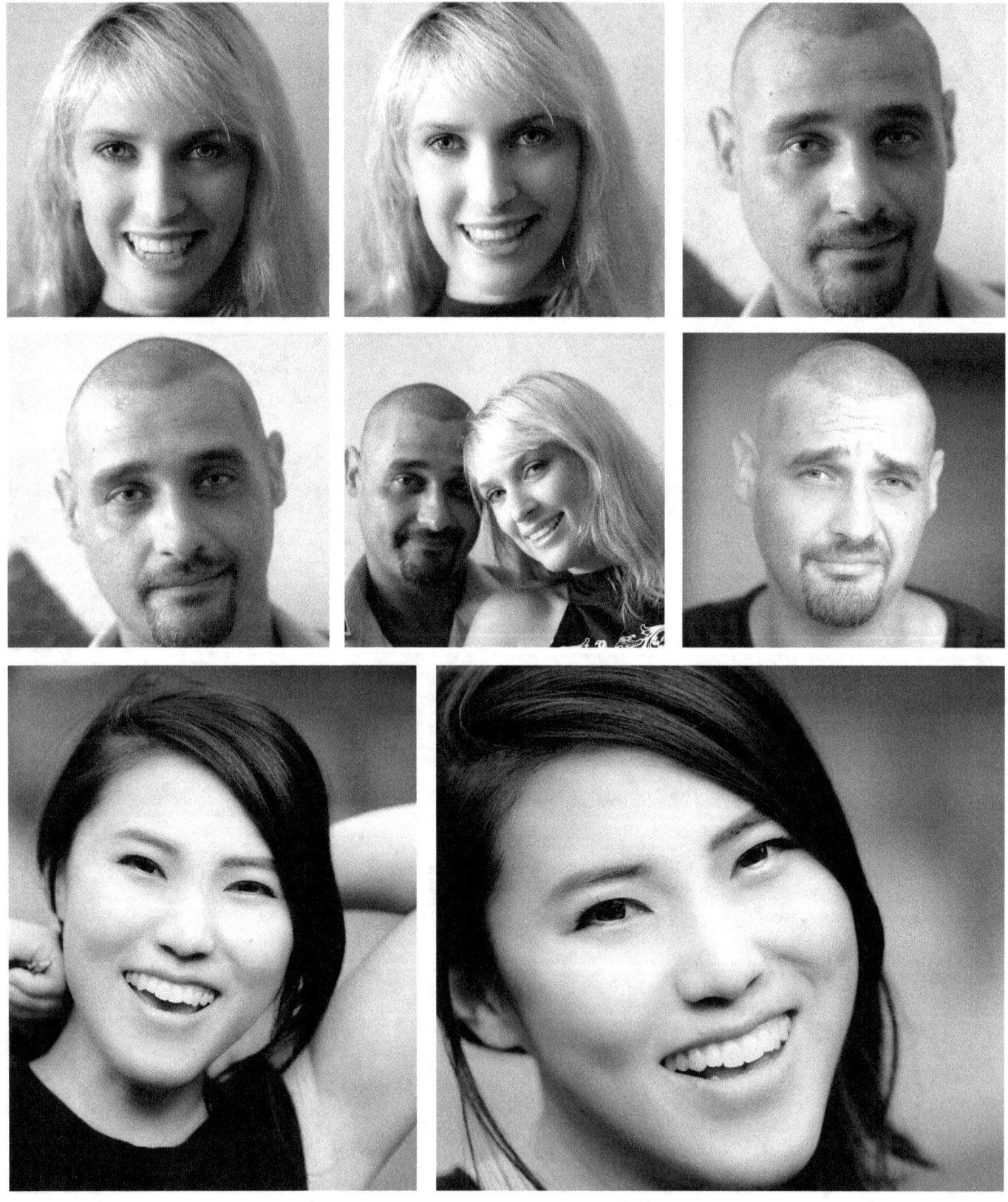

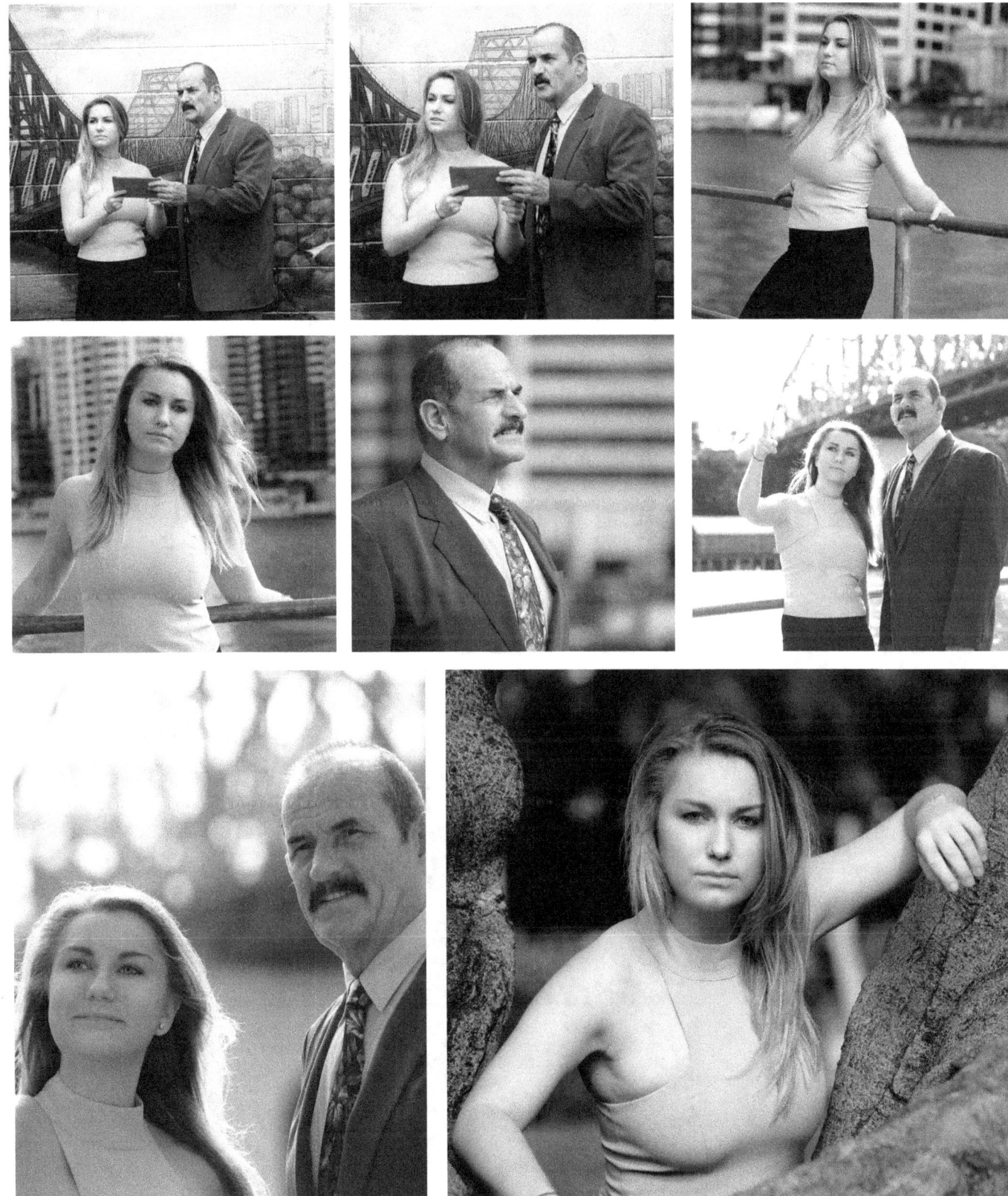

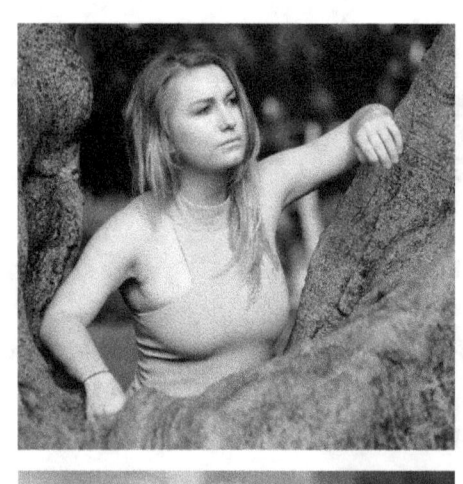
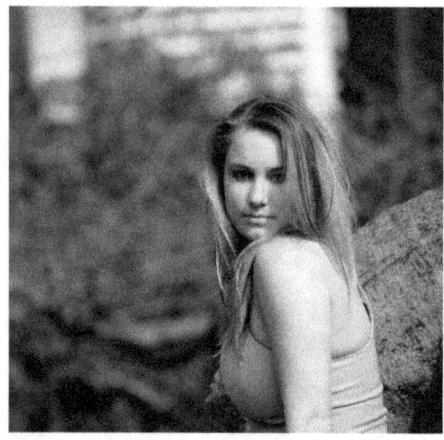
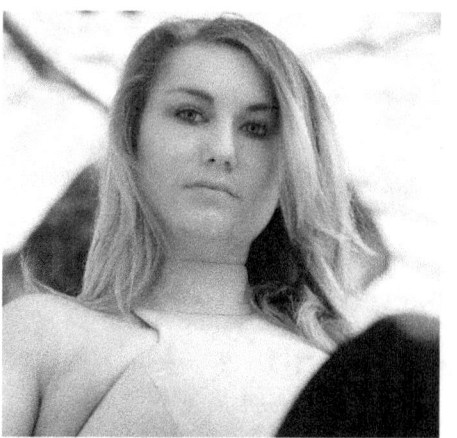
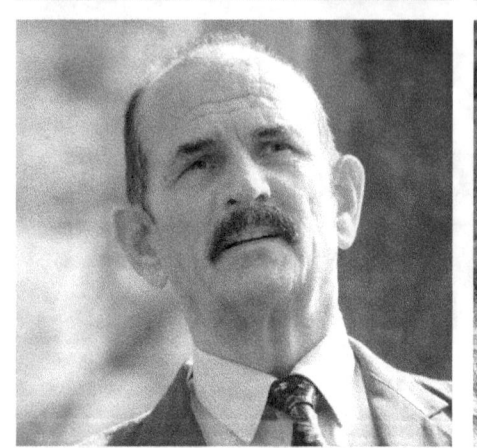
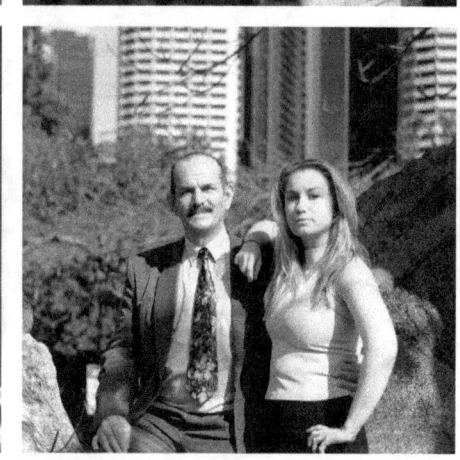
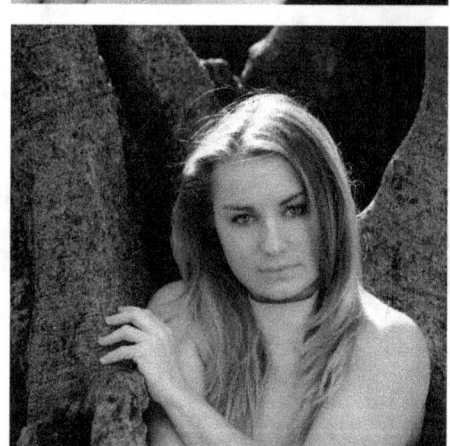
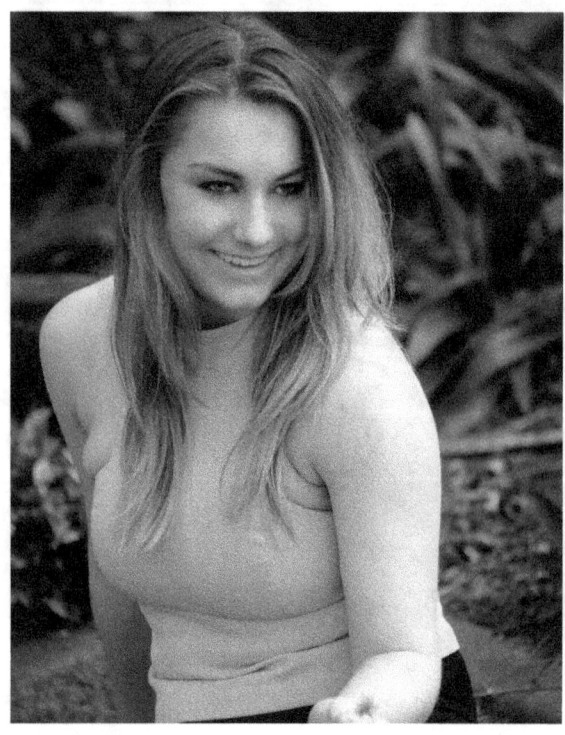
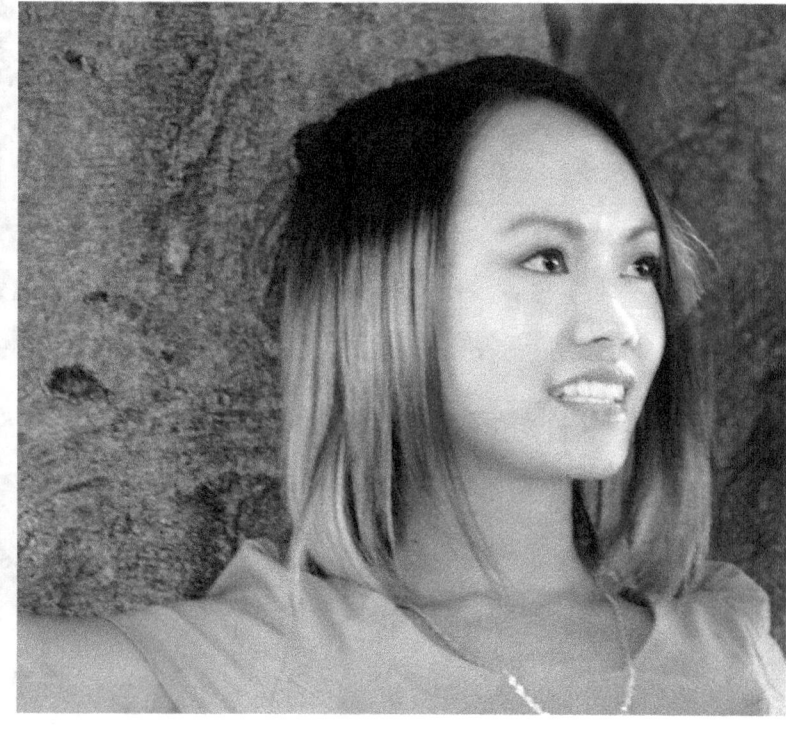

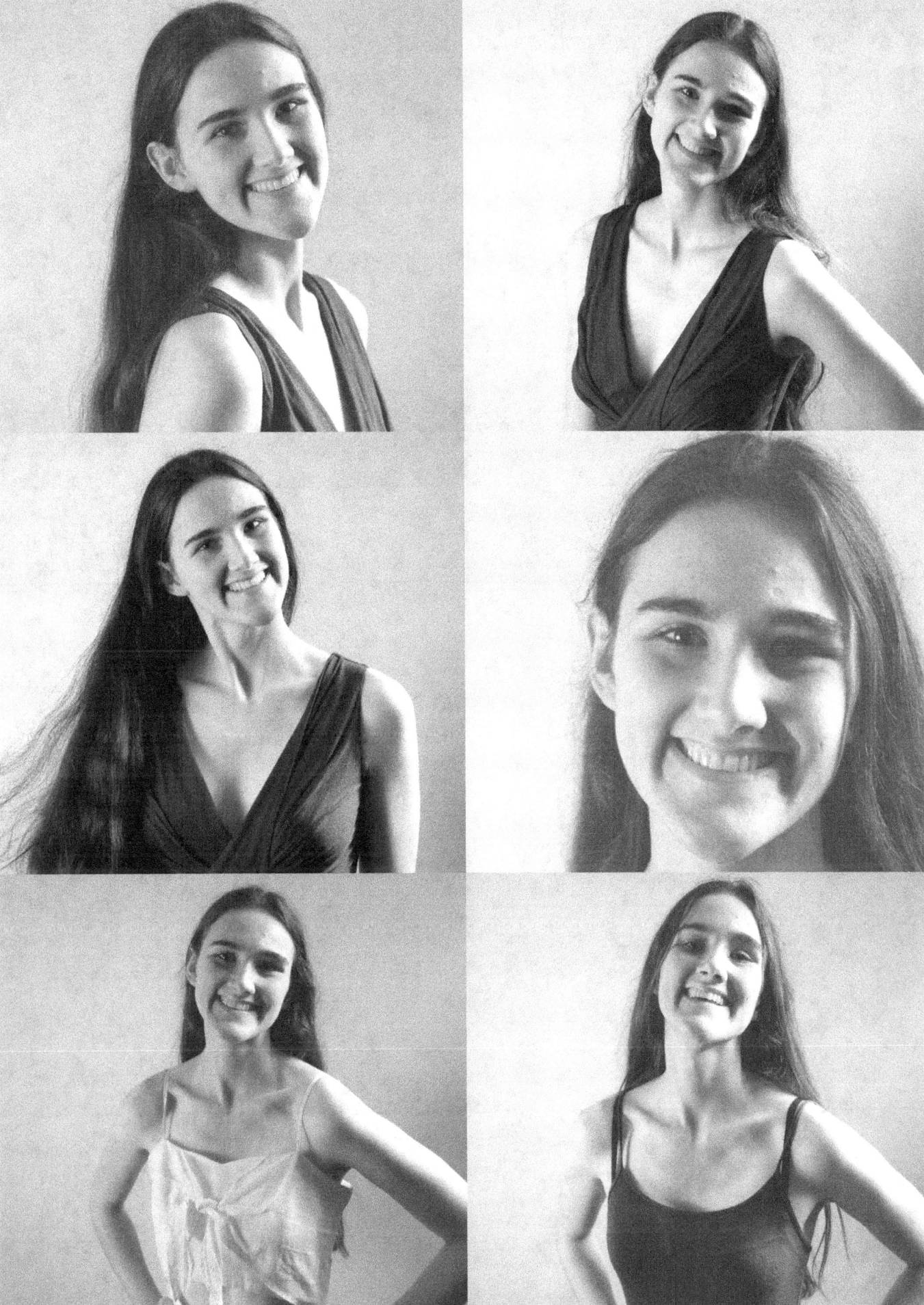

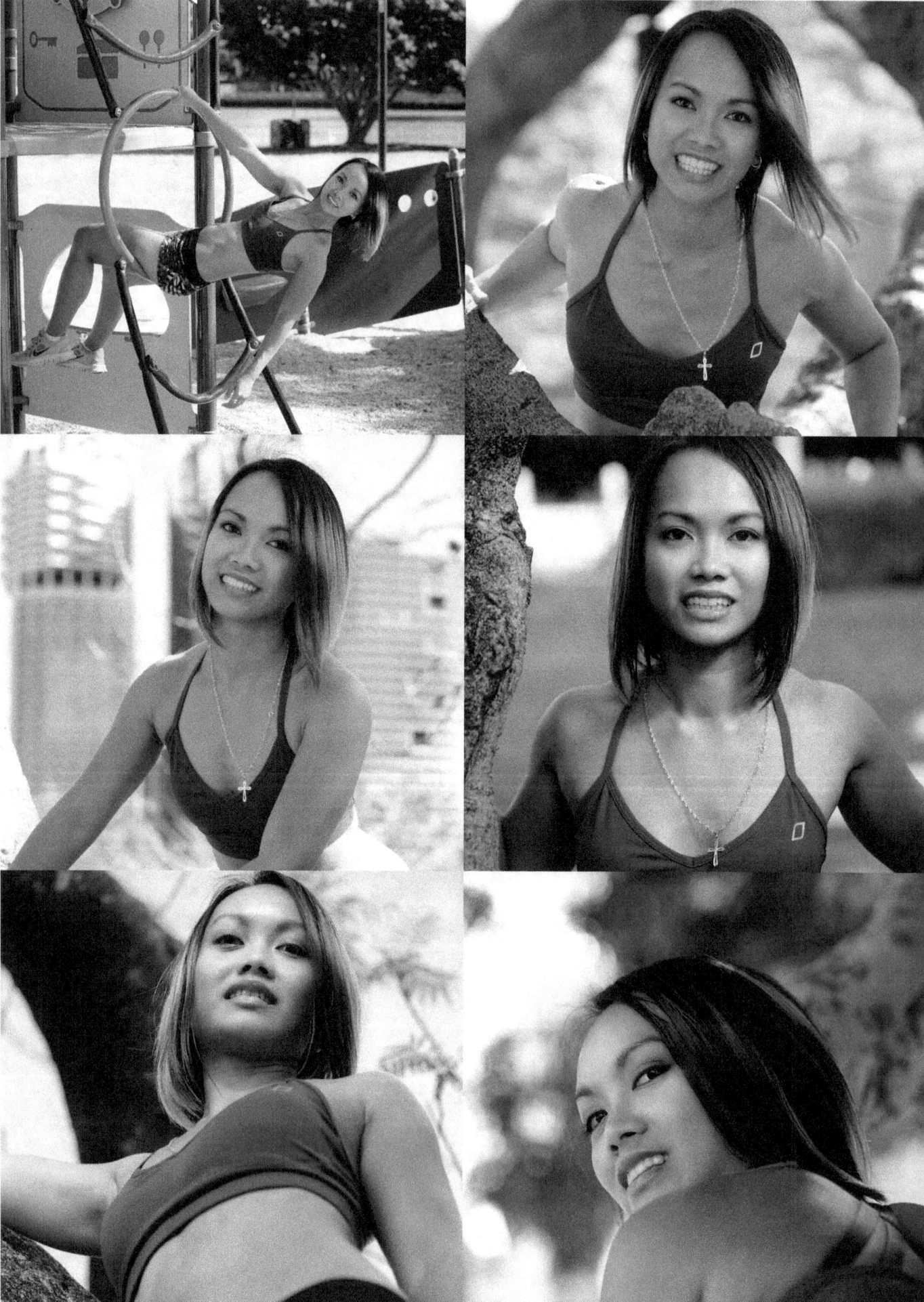

John Burke Park
pages 45 to 49 inclusive

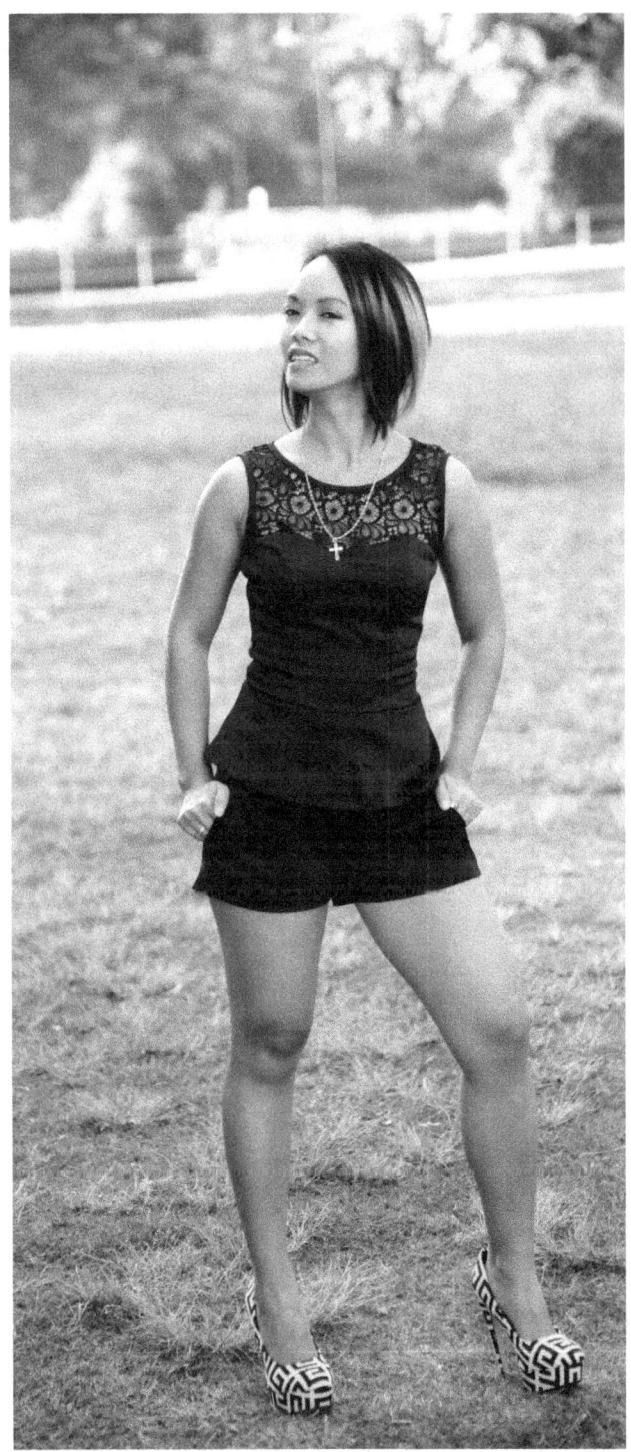

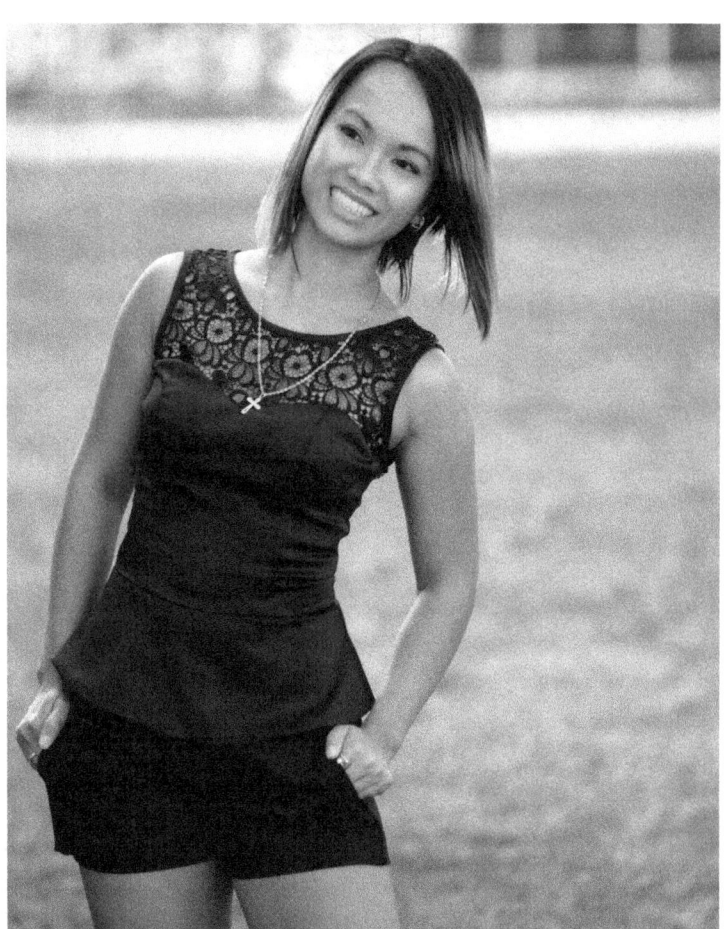

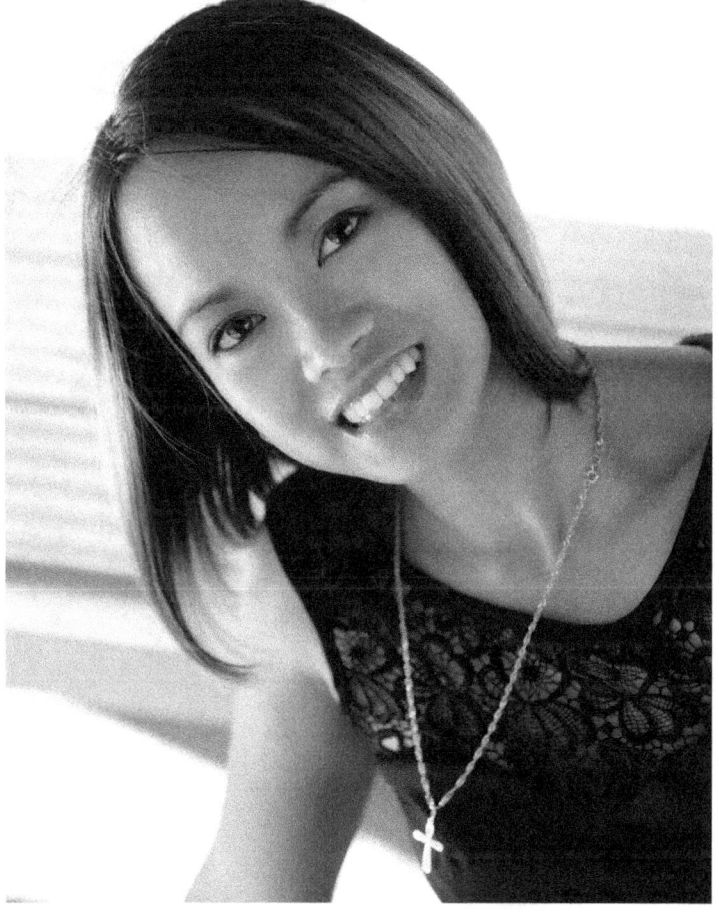

page 49

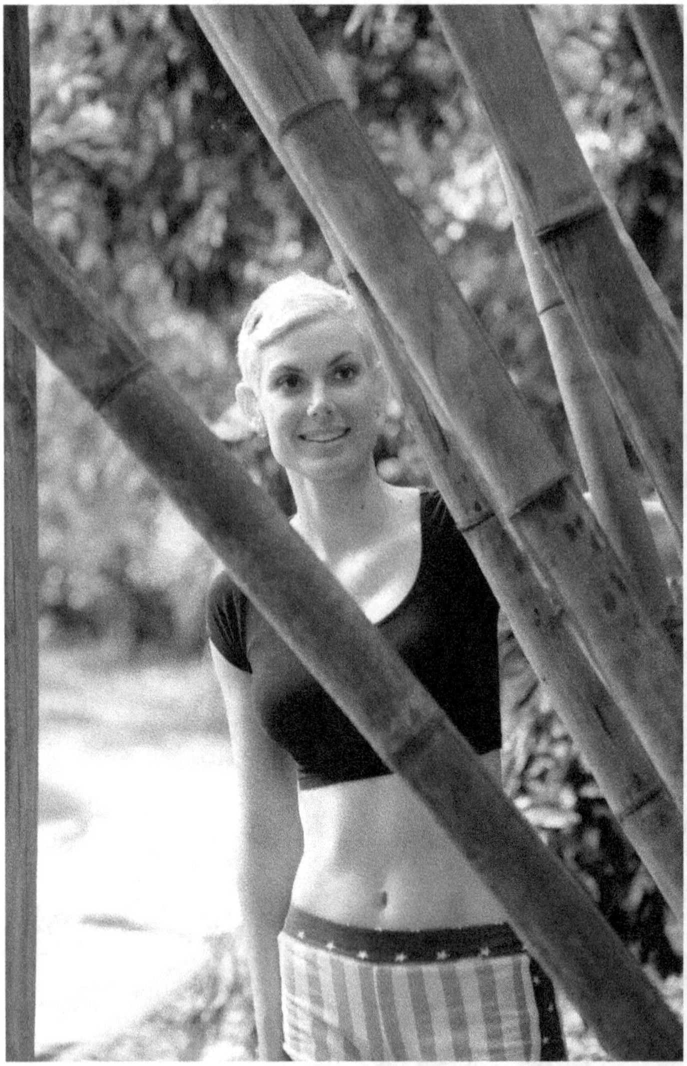

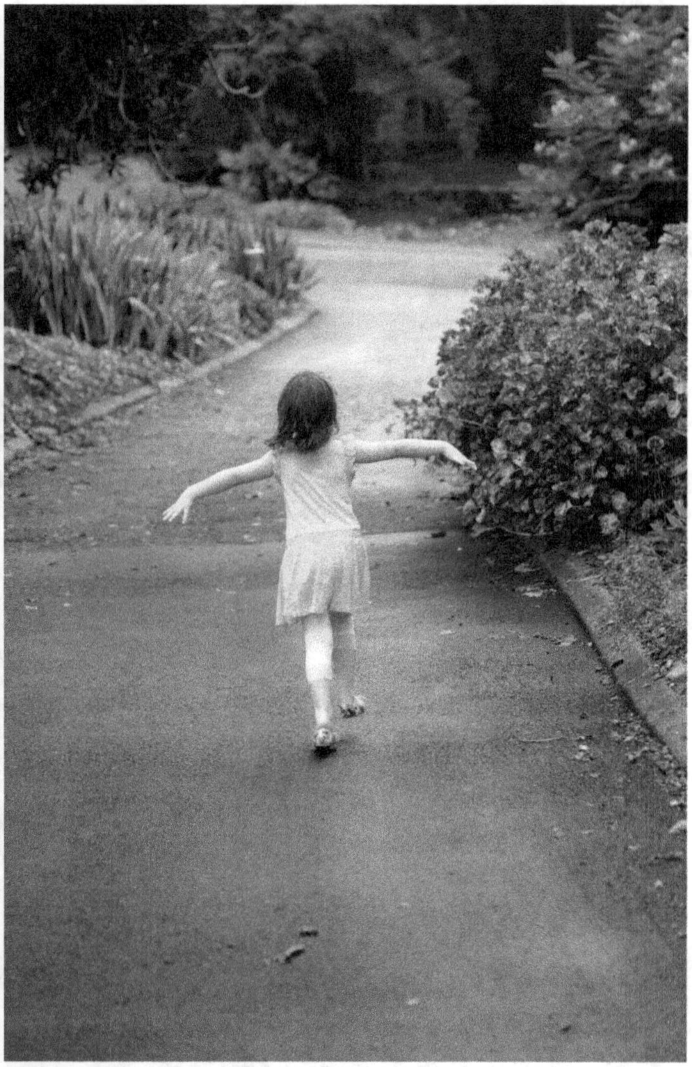

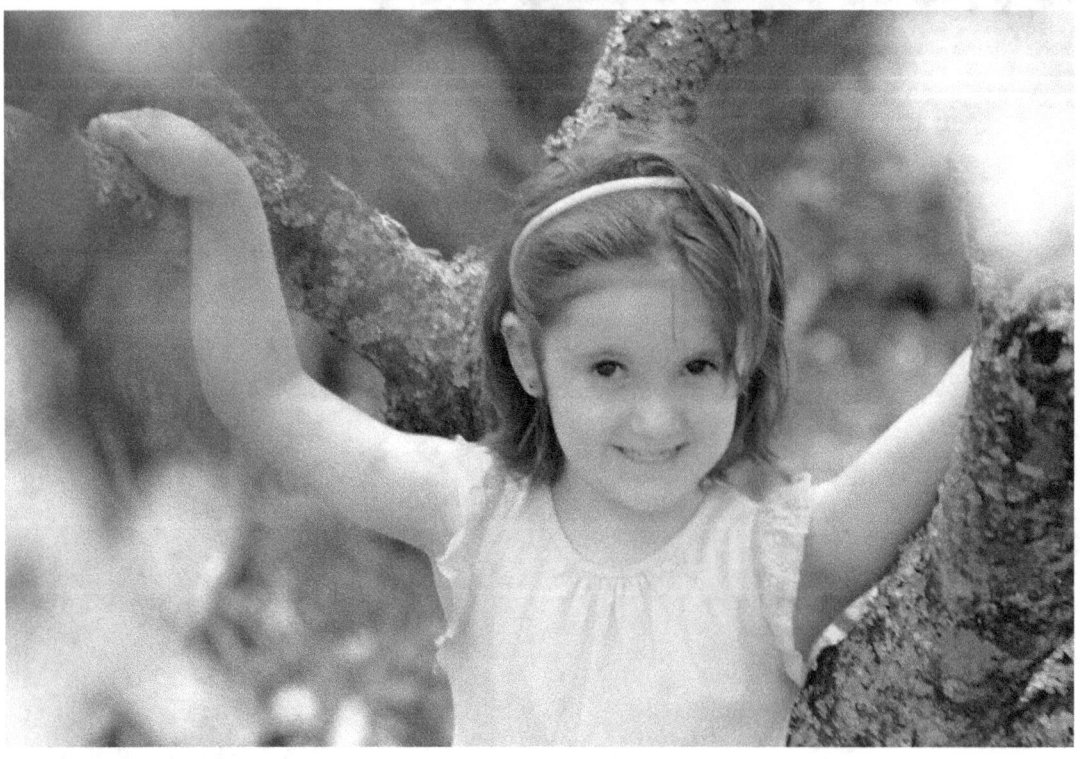

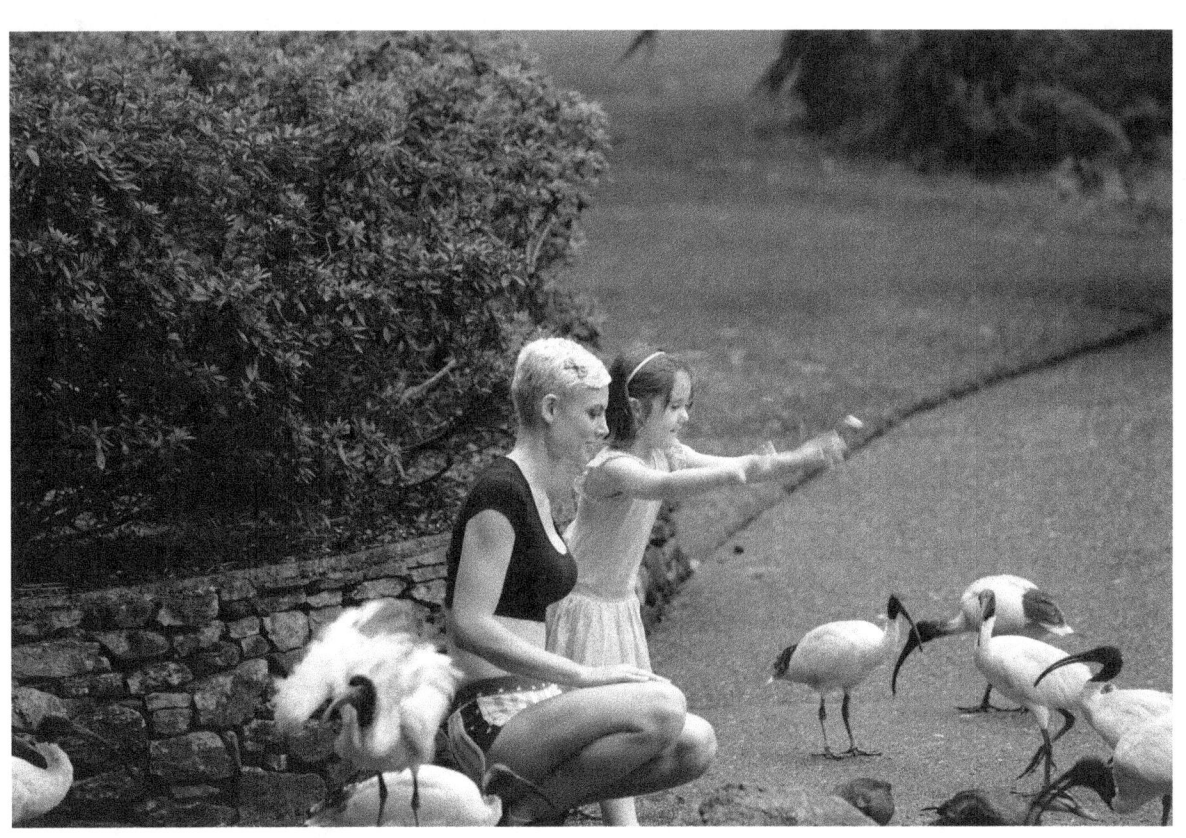

My Coot-tha Botanic Gardens pages 50 and 51

page 51

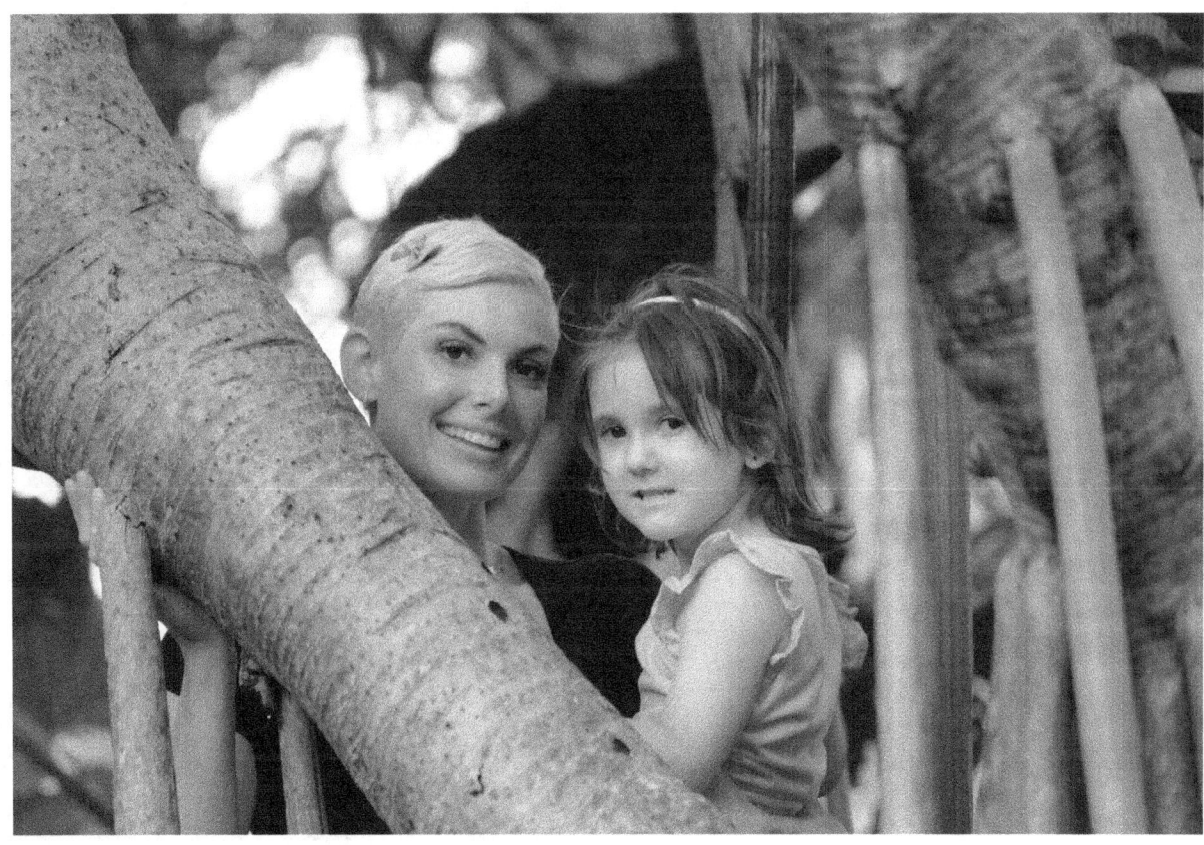

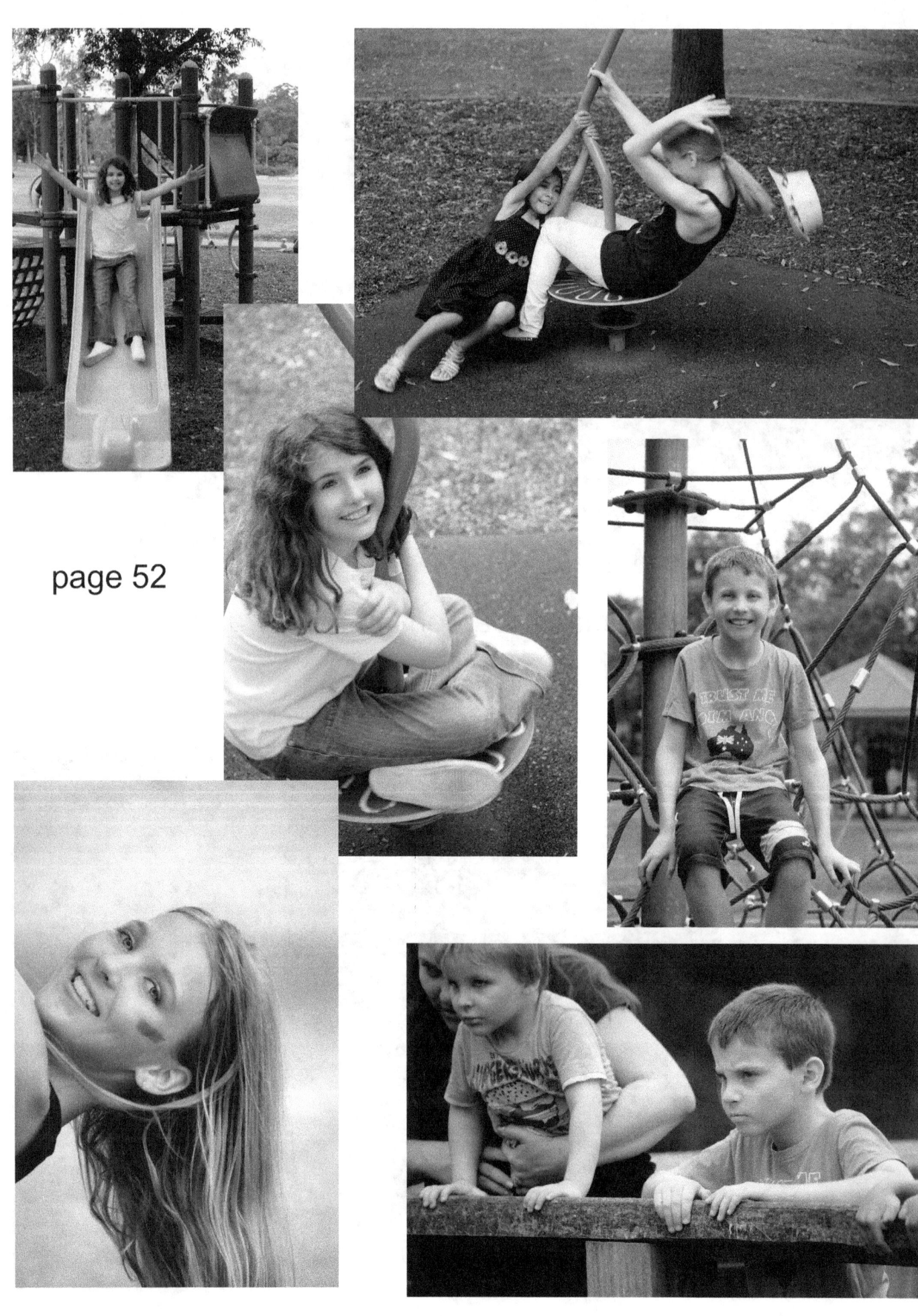

page 52